I0560687

It Had To Happen:
What's A Man Without A Legacy?

Dr. Kareem "DJ Kayotik" Thomson

With Dee "lilD" Porter

LLTK Publishing

Published by LLTK Publishing

ISBN: 979-8-9930861-0-1 (Hardcover)
ISBN: 979-8-9930861-1-8 (Paperback)
ISBN: 979-8-9930861-2-5 (Audiobook-Digital Download)
ISBN: 979-8-9930861-3-2 (Kindle)

First Edition

DEDICATION

This book is dedicated to the memory of my son, **DANTE AKEE THOMSON**.

It's been **10 long years** since you tragically left us.
Still unbelievable.
This pain doesn't feel like a decade has passed—it feels like it happened **10 days... 10 hours... 10 minutes... 10 seconds ago**.

Life as I knew it **changed suddenly**, right before my eyes.
Things will never be the same.
When a parent loses a child, it leaves a permanent hole in the heart—
My heart will forever be broken.

I didn't just lose my *son*...
I lost my hopes.
I lost my dreams.
I lost my legacy.
I lost everything I wanted—and more than words could ever express.

The hardest thing I've ever had to hear: **"Your son is gone."**
The hardest thing I've ever had to do: **live every day since that moment.**

By the grace of God, my **faith** has covered and carried me.
It's given me the courage, the strength, and the transparency to finally share:

My story.
My tears.
My pain.
My purpose.
My testimony.

I pray God continues to give me the strength to keep going—
And that your memories keep sustaining me.

Thank you, DANTE, for not only being my *son*, but also my *angel in heaven*,
motivating me to be the man I am today.

Until I see you again...
#LongLiveTheKidd

CONTENTS

FOREWORD
by Curtis "50 Cent" Jackson

Legacy ain't something you get handed—it's something you fight for. It's built in silence, in pain, in moments when nobody's watching and everything's on the line. I've seen a lot in my life—growing up in Southside Jamaica, Queens, you learn quick that nothing comes easy. But even in a place known for hard knocks, there are some stories that stand out. Kareem Thomson's is one of them.

I've known Kareem since we were kids—back before the deals, the fame, the world tours. Back when all we had were dreams, and Southside was a war zone during the crack era. Back when survival was the win. Even then, Kareem had something different about him. A quiet strength. A realness that couldn't be faked.

Years later, when we reconnected, I already knew he had turned himself into DJ Kayotik—rocking crowds across the globe, building a name. But I didn't know the full weight of what he carried to get there. Behind the lights, the beats, and the stages, there was a storm—one that would've broken most men.

Kareem lived through things that would shake your soul. Homelessness. Abuse. Loss. And the hardest pain a father could ever face—the death of his only son, Dante. That kind of pain can bury you. It almost buried him. But instead of folding, he found something deep inside—a reason to keep going.

That's what this book is about. It's not just about music or fame. It's about survival. It's about finding your purpose in the middle of your pain. It's about what it means to take every hit life throws and still stand up swinging. That's legacy.

It Had To Happen: What's A Man Without A Legacy is more than a title—it's the truth. Kareem's story is a mirror for anybody who's ever felt like giving up. And proof that you can take the worst chapters of your life and still write something powerful.

This ain't just a book. It's a reminder that strength doesn't come from avoiding the fire—it comes from walking through it and coming out the other side still standing. That's what Kareem did. And that's why his story matters.

—Curtis "50 Cent" Jackson

ACKNOWLEDGMENTS

First and foremost, I express my deepest gratitude to **God**—for His unwavering strength, guidance, and inspiration that made the completion of this book possible. His grace has been my constant source of healing and motivation throughout this journey. I am humbled to dedicate both my life and this work to His glory.

To my superhero, my mother **Rosalie Jackson**—your unwavering love and limitless support have carried me through every chapter of life and every page of this book. Your faith in me has been my anchor, my fuel, and the foundation on which this story stands. Thank you for raising me with strength, sacrifice, and love— and for shaping me into the man I am today.

To my beloved wife, **Vanessa Rose-Thomson**—thank you for your unwavering support, patience, and inspiration throughout the writing process. You read the drafts, offered honest feedback, and stood by me through every painful memory and every revision—not just of this book, but of me. Thank you for your grace, your strength, your love, and for always being my biggest cheerleader.

To my beautiful daughters, **Jewel Thomson** and **Jayla Thomson**—you are my heartbeat, both inside and out. Your love, laughter, and light gave me the strength to keep going, even when I wanted to give up. Every word of this book was written with you in mind, and every page carries a piece of my heart for you.

To my bonus son, **Jawaun Rose-Buie**—thank you for opening your heart and allowing me to be part of your world. Your acceptance not only deepened our bond but helped knit our family together. I'm grateful for your love, your presence, and the authenticity you bring into our lives. Thank you for being unapologetically you.

To my bonus dad, **William Jackson** (aka Pops)—I once promised my mother I'd retire her so she could finally relax and enjoy life. Then you came into our lives—and beat me to it. From the moment we met, you've loved her, and me, with a full and unconditional heart. I'm truly honored to call you "Pops," and even more grateful to witness the joy and peace you've brought to her life.

To my incredible mother-in-law, **Gloria Rose**—thank you for welcoming me into your family with open arms, unwavering love, and God-centered grace. Your prayers, your wisdom, and your quiet strength have been a blessing to my journey. I am truly honored to be your son-in-law, and I thank God for your presence in my life. I love you dearly.

To my brother from another mother, **Dwight "Bunkin" Parham**—you know the chapters I didn't write, because you lived them with me. From Southside kids chasing daylight to grown men standing in the fire and coming out stronger, our bond has been battle-tested and never wavered. Thank you for walking beside me when I could've easily walked alone. Your loyalty, your laughter, your presence—it all means more than words can say. KABU 4 Life, my brother. Always.

To **Nikita Fridia**, Dante's mother—thank you for blessing me with the greatest gift of my life: our son. You raised Dante with unwavering love, strength, and purpose for 18 incredible years. Even in the face of unimaginable loss, you continue to pour into our family with grace—as godmother to Jewel and Jayla, and as a steady presence in our lives. Dante's love and legacy gave rise to a beautifully blended family that I believe reflects God's divine plan. Though we grieve differently, we grieve together—forever connected by the love of a son who changed our lives. Thank you for your strength, your support, and your contributions to this book and to our shared journey.

To **Brandice Williams**—the friend who became family. Your love and encouragement have shaped me in ways I can't fully express. Thank you for being godmother to Dante, Jewel, and Jayla—and for being a guiding light through our darkest days. You are a true example of what friendship really means.

To **Dorothea "DC" Cole**—your strength, heart, and unwavering support have meant the world to me. From your presence at Dante's wake to the countless prayers you've lifted on my behalf, you've been more than a friend—you've been family.

Now, we share a pain no parent should ever have to carry. Losing a child changes everything, and only those who've walked through that fire truly understand. I want you to know that I see you, I honor you, and I carry your son's name in my heart along with my own. May our angels rest in peace, and may we continue to find purpose in their memory. Thank you for standing with me then—and now.

To my brother, **Curtis "50 Cent" Jackson** — thank you not only for writing the foreword to this book, but for believing in me and my story when I needed it most. Your unwavering support, guidance, and example of turning vision into legacy have been a constant reminder of what's possible through faith, discipline, and hustle. Beyond the stages and the spotlight, your brotherhood means more than words can express. I'm deeply grateful for everything you've done for me and my family.

To my cousin, **Caryn Boyd**—thank you for your unwavering support, steady encouragement, and quiet strength throughout this journey. You've always been there, rooting for me in ways both seen and unseen. I love you deeply, Cuzzo—always have, always will.

To **Dray Williams**—brother, business manager, and now Vice President of The Kayotik Foundation. From day one, your belief in the vision helped lay the foundation for everything we've built together. Your loyalty has never wavered, your leadership continues to inspire, and your brotherhood means the world to me. I'm truly grateful to have you in my corner.

To my brother, **Chad "BC" Newton**—two decades of wins, losses, and growth. You've been a business partner, a friend, and family to me and mine. Thank you for your love, loyalty, and commitment to this ride we're still on.

To **Wanda Hardeman**, my former therapist and now family— this book would not exist without you. You saved me. You held up the mirror and helped me see both the broken boy and the man I had become. You taught me how to communicate, how to unpack trauma, and how to grow. Your lessons continue to shape me into a better father, husband, and man. I'm still growing—and I thank you for that.

To **Pastor Rickie G. Rush**—your unwavering faith and powerful walk with God have profoundly impacted my life. When my son passed, you stepped in and made it a point to be my Cornerman—covering me in prayer, encouragement, and presence when I needed it most. Your wisdom, your faith, and your example have guided me through some of my darkest moments. Thank you for being a true man of God and a steady light in my corner.

To my extended family and friends—thank you for being there when I didn't believe in myself. To all who contributed directly or indirectly to this project—you know who you are—your love and support have been priceless.

To **Dee "lilD" Porter**—thank you for bringing my story to life with care, courage, and clarity. I truly believe God handpicked you to walk this journey beside me, and I'm beyond grateful He did. You gave me space to be vulnerable, challenged me with love, and honored my voice with authenticity. You didn't just help me write a book—you helped me tell my truth. You are the real MVP. Thank you for every word, every hour, and every ounce of belief you poured into this process.

A special thanks to **Dr. K.C. Fox** and the editorial team at **PullCorp Media & Business Consulting Group**—thank you for guiding me through this publishing journey with care, wisdom, and professionalism. Your insights, patience, and unwavering belief in this project helped shape this manuscript into something I'm truly proud to share with the world.

Finally, to the readers—thank you for picking up this book and giving my story a space in your hands and heart. If even one sentence resonates with your journey, then this mission was worth it. For everyone who finds a piece of themselves in these pages, I pray you walk away with strength, healing, and unshakable hope. May you be reminded that nothing in life is wasted when you walk in purpose—and that every setback, every scar, and every storm can still lead to legacy.

Thank you for breathing life into this journey.
I am forever grateful.

CHAPTER 1
"THEY CAN'T FIND HIM..."

"Dante jumped into a lake…they can't find him."

What did you just say to me?

What do you mean they can't find my firstborn?

They can't find my only son?

Nah, I must've heard her wrong.

I'd just DJ'd the night before and was still in bed, halfway between dreams and reality. My head wasn't clear yet. There's no way she said what I think she said. The confusion hit me like a ton of bricks—disbelief flooding my entire body. So I asked her to repeat it, needing clarity, even though I already knew I'd never forget those words.

And again, Dante's mom, Nikita, said the sentence that shattered my soul: "They. Can't. Find. Him."

I froze in place, like time had stopped.

Unfortunately, I wasn't there for my son's birth. I met Nikita while I was stationed in Virginia during my time in the Navy. When she got pregnant, she made the decision to return to her hometown in East Texas. I didn't follow her. At just 22 years old, I wasn't ready to be someone's father—yet I was determined to be nothing like mine.

Still, I had mixed feelings about moving to Texas to be a full-time dad and family man. You gotta understand—Nikita's from a small city in East Texas. I'm from the biggest, baddest city in the country. The city that never sleeps. The Big Apple. And all I kept telling myself was: "There's no way I'm moving to the country to be surrounded by cows and horses."

But despite the doubts and cultural whiplash, one thing was never in question: I was going to be there for my son. The moment he came into this world, I made that promise to myself.

Dante decided to make his entrance a little early, so I got to him the very next day—March 9, 1997. The same day Biggie died.

Of course. As a true New Yorker, it made perfect sense that I would meet my firstborn on the day one of our greatest legends was taken from us. It was like the city and my story would forever be linked by both birth and death.

Back in East Texas, I was officially a father. I remember that day like it was yesterday. Not only did I meet my son for the first time, but I also met Nikita's family. Her crazy uncles picked me up from the airport and gave me a warm, if not slightly suspicious, welcome into their world. They were still trying to figure out how the hell this loud New York dude managed to steal their niece's heart and now had her having a baby. They joked the entire ride, even suggested stopping for drinks, but they knew all I wanted was to get to the hospital and see my son and check on his mother.

To this day, I'll always appreciate how her entire family embraced me. They're the definition of true Southern hospitality— warm, raw, and real.

Dante Akee Thomson—my son, my legacy—shared both my middle and last name. And he would know, without a doubt, that his daddy loved him. The only reason I moved to Dallas was to be close to him. Over the years, after some hard lessons and growing up, we built a relationship where we talked every day and saw each other often—even though we were nearly three hours apart.

I'll never forget the day he called me to share his college decision. I was at the radio station, standing in the kitchen making coffee, when my phone rang.

"I'ma be a Lumberjack," he said.

Stephen F. Austin University. Solid choice. Smart move. Dante had three clear career paths in front of him: take over for me and carry on the DJ legacy, open a luxury sneaker resale boutique, or become a pharmacist like his big cousin Deshanda. SFA has a phenomenal pharmacy program, and he was already known for having the most exclusive kicks. The store idea just needed space and opportunity. And since he'd already been booking DJ gigs, putting me up on new music, and growing a name of his own, I knew he'd be up next.

He was my legacy in motion—my future echoing back at me.

The kind of love I had for my son, my father never gave me. But my mother did. So I figured, if I could simply be the opposite of him, maybe I could be the kind of parent my son deserved.

Dante and I had only recently rebuilt the bond we were always supposed to have. That connection had been strained years earlier when I married someone who wasn't his mother. I was stubborn, a Taurus through and through. I expected him to be happy for me. I thought he was just siding with his mom and not considering my perspective. But the truth is—he was a child. A twelve-year-old boy. It was never his job to fix what the adults broke.

When I was his age, my mother was playing both roles in the house. I used to tell people, "My mother is my father." Whether my dad was physically there or not, he was absent in every way that mattered. He didn't provide a blueprint for fatherhood—hell, for life. He gave me nothing but disappointment, confusion, and emotional baggage that would eventually be unpacked in therapy. Everything I knew about parenting came from my mom, and from the trial-and-error of on-the-job training.

And honestly? From Vanessa.

My wife stayed on my ass about rebuilding my relationship with Dante. She held me accountable, lovingly but firmly, until I responded to him with the maturity and humility he deserved.

Vanessa saw the best in me, even when I couldn't see it in myself, and she pushed me—daily—to become that version of me.

Over time, not only did my relationship with Dante deepen, but his bond with Vanessa grew as well. He loved his little sisters—Jewel and Jayla, our daughters—with a big brother's pride. They adored him right back.

A big reason Dante became a DJ was to be closer to me. He wanted to walk in my footsteps. We even picked his name together. At first, we asked my mom—she named me DJ Kayotik, beginning and ending with a "K." The acronym? Kareem's Alternative Youth Options To Improve Kids. That later inspired my 501(c)(3) nonprofit, The Kayotik Foundation, launched in 2011.

If my mom could come up with something that powerful, I knew she'd think of something fly for Dante too. She suggested DJ Light, based on Matthew 5:16—"In the same way, let your light shine before others, that they may see your good deeds and glorify your Father in heaven."

Beautiful verse. But Dante wasn't feeling it. So I suggested DJ Kid. He added the extra "d" for "DJ Kid Dante," and became known as DJ Kidd.

A few months before Nikita's call, DJ Kidd had a gig in Deep Ellum, a bustling part of downtown Dallas filled with clubs, lounges, food spots, and rooftop energy. During that party, someone was shot and killed. Dante wasn't a suspect—he was a witness. But the police detained him anyway, trying to gather details. Nikita called me in a panic.

"Come get your son. Come get him now."

Our co-parenting had never been better. We had grown closer—healing, forgiving, trusting again. She knew I was 35 minutes away, and she didn't have to ask twice. She called, I came. That's what real fathers do.

Did he see the shooter?

Did the shooter see him?

Would they think he snitched?

I didn't want Dante caught up in any of that mess. I told him on the phone, "Don't say a word. I'm on my way." That's what protection looks like. That's what presence looks like. That's what parenting looks like.

Back to the moment.

Vanessa had just come in from shopping with her mom. She was about to eat when I repeated what Nikita told me. She dropped her fork. "WHAT? I don't understand. What do you mean, they can't find him?"

The love I have for my Jamaican, Gemini queen goes back to 1990 at Jamaica High School, better known as "The Beaverdome," on 167-01 Gothic Drive in Queens. Life back then? Rough. Heavy. Chaotic. My childhood? A battlefield.

If the worst thing I endured was having a father addicted to crack and a mother addicted to her man, maybe—just maybe—I could've had some kind of normal. But my trauma went deeper. Relatives who turned their backs on me. Dreams stolen—literally and figuratively—by the people who were supposed to protect me. We'll get to all that.

But Vanessa saw through all of it. She saw Kareem when I was broke, starving, and angry. I refused to hustle the poison that was killing my family, even though it meant staying broke. I needed another way—a righteous way—to help my mom. And Vanessa Rose saw that in me.

I'll never forget being 15, stomach growling in class, and asking her to bring me something from the bodega. Asking your girl to feed you? That's a whole different kind of humbling. She didn't judge me. She brought me that egg and cheese on a bagel.

But at that moment, hearing that my son was missing, I'd rather have been hungry than heartbroken.

Vanessa kept repeating, "I don't understand."

I finally snapped: "THEY CAN'T FIND HIM!"

I was incoherent. Paralyzed by panic. Frantic.

Unlike my father, who never showed concern when I was hurt or missing, I was gripped with terror at the thought of losing my child. When my mom once told him the doctor had to stitch my head back together, it barely moved him. Me? I couldn't breathe.

The idea of never seeing my son again made my entire body shut down. That kind of agony? My father never knew it. But I did.

And I'm not here to bash him. I've learned the power of forgiveness. Addiction stole my father from me long before death did in 2018. I just wish I'd had the chance to say, "I forgive you."

Maybe that was his purpose in my life—to show me everything I'd never be. And every day, I reminded myself: I will not be him.

Vanessa saw I wasn't okay. "Get in the car," she said. "I'm driving." My mind was racing. My heart pounding. I couldn't sit still. All I knew was: my son needed me. And I had to get to him. Nothing else mattered.

Vanessa's mother was home and thank God for her. She stayed with Jewel and Jayla until the nanny arrived. Jewel was four. Jayla was two. And even in the middle of chaos, we couldn't leave Grandma alone too long with those two beautiful, energetic firecrackers.

But in that moment, all I could think was: Please God, let my son be okay!

CHAPTER 2
"DADDY TOOK MY MONEY…"

My mom told me the story of my birth like it was a love story. It was a special day for her and my father—they were about to welcome their first child together. It was Saturday, April 26, 1975, in Queens, New York. While rushing to the hospital, my father almost ended up delivering me in the back of a cab.

But Moms wasn't going out like that. Queens in the mid-70s was alive with grit and soul—block parties, bell bottoms, and a sense of pride even in the struggle. That's the world I was born into.

"I am not having this damn baby in this dirty-ass cab," she said.

Luckily, I was born at Queens General Hospital. My father had picked out this beautiful flower arrangement shaped like a poodle, and my mom lit up. She said not only did she experience love at first sight when I arrived, but she got to share that moment with the love of her life. My mother loved my father deeply. He was her first boyfriend. Her first love. Her first everything. And that connection—that bond between them—stuck around for a long time, even when it probably shouldn't have.

Fast forward to when I was five years old. We had just moved to Corona, Queens. I ended up in the hospital again—this time not for birth, but for stitches. And not just a few. We're talking head trauma.

Now look, kids get into things. Scrapes, bruises—that's just part of growing up. But there's no excuse for a five-year-old's brain to be peeking out of his skull.

It was 1980—the so-called good old days.

My mom was hot-combing her hair and didn't want me inhaling the chemical fumes, so she asked my father to take me outside and watch me for a while. I went out. But he didn't. He ended up in someone else's apartment in the same building. I was left outside—alone, in a new neighborhood I didn't know, surrounded by kids I didn't recognize.

That's when four older kids spotted me and decided to make me their afternoon entertainment. They convinced me to climb into a manhole. It wasn't fully covered—just one of those grated openings that should've been sealed during the building renovations. I was small, curious, and unsupervised. All bad combinations.

Maybe if my father had been there, he would've spotted the danger. Maybe he would've stopped me. But he wasn't. So I climbed in. But almost as soon as I got down there, something in my little brain told me this wasn't where I was supposed to be. Get out. I started climbing back up, but just as I reached the top, the biggest of the boys dropped the metal cover onto my head.

I blacked out for a moment. When I came to, two of the boys were pulling me out and walking me home. My face was covered in blood and dirt. I couldn't see clearly, but I knew something was wrong. I could feel it. The blood was warm and steady. I could feel it dripping down my face. It was everywhere. They pounded on our apartment door like the police.

My mother opened it and instantly lost her mind. She screamed. Not just out of fear—but out of rage, panic, helplessness. She didn't even know where the blood was coming from. It was just... gushing. After a few seconds of scrambling, she figured it out. She grabbed a towel and tried to stop the bleeding. Then she threw on some clothes, grabbed her purse, and we jumped in a cab—headed right back to Queens General. I remember her hands trembling as she pressed a towel against my head, whispering prayers while holding back tears. The cab ride felt like forever, every bump on the road sending a fresh jolt of pain through my skull.

And my father? The same man who held me at birth? Was nowhere to be found. At the hospital, social services questioned my mom. "How does a five-year-old get a head wound like this?"

"Where were you?" "Where was his father?" I was too young to speak up for her, but I wanted to. I wanted to tell them everything. About how she was just trying to comb her hair, about how she told him to watch me, and how he chose not to. But yeah, I would've like to known...where was my dad?

They gave me twelve stitches. Twelve. The doctor said I might suffer brain damage because I had been left untreated for too long. But physically, I healed. Emotionally, something shifted. That day, I learned my father couldn't be trusted to show up.

When we got home, my mom went off. She cursed him out for being irresponsible, for being selfish, for not protecting his son. And what did he do? He acted like it wasn't a big deal. Like nothing had happened. No apology. No guilt. No real concern.

I watched the whole thing and quietly made a decision: I'll never be like him. If I ever had a son, he would know what it feels like to be protected. To have someone watching over him. That would be my job.

After the dust settled, my mom put on her cape and went into full action mode. Because of the apartment complex's negligence— leaving that manhole exposed during renovations—she filed a lawsuit. And we won. It wasn't life-changing money, but as she called it, "a nice little piece of change." About $2,500. Enough for us to move to a better place.

We ended up in Rochdale Village—130th and Guy R Brewer Blvd in Southside Jamaica, Queens. Rochdale was technically still the projects, but it felt more like a community. People knew each other. Looked out for each other. Rent stayed consistent. And there was pride in ownership—Moms liked that.

We had great times in Rochdale. I remember playing skully in the streets—an old NYC game with bottle caps and chalk-drawn boards. We'd play for hours. Sometimes for fun, sometimes for money. And then came Christmas of 1982. Man, that was the one.

My dad was working as a security guard, making decent money—$18 or $19 an hour. My mom had good credit and a steady job. WBLS had Frankie Crocker spinning Christmas classics. The house smelled like food and love. We didn't have a turkey—we had Cornish hen, flour gravy, rice, spinach, canned corn, cranberry sauce, Christmas candy—it was all there. And the gifts? Crazy.

I got the original Nintendo with Duck Hunt—the one with the orange gun. Super Mario Bros. Double Dribble. But the crown jewel? A big, blue mountain bike. New York Giants blue. It was beautiful. And it was mine.

Three days later, it was gone. Not because a group of boys jumped me. Nah. It was worse. A girl stole it. She was taller, heavier, and definitely older. She walked up to me while I was riding on the dirt mounds—the "mountains" we used for stunts—and said,

"That's a nice bike."

"Thanks."

"Can I ride it?"

"My mom and dad said I can't let anybody hold it."

"I just wanna test it. I'm thinking about getting one."

Against my better judgment, I let her. She rode in circles for a few seconds. Then she took off. Gone. I chased her all the way to Section 1. But by the time I got there, it was too late. I couldn't breathe. My heart was pounding. My bike—the best gift I'd ever gotten—was gone.

I told co-op security. My mom and dad came rushing out, hopping fences trying to help me. I appreciated them for that. But there was nothing they could do. She was gone. So was my bike. I felt violated. I felt stupid. But mostly, I felt helpless.

That's when Moms signed me up for martial arts at the Rochdale Community Center. That's where I met Sensei Robert Wallace. He changed my life.

He didn't just teach me how to fight. He taught me control, focus, and discipline. He became the father figure I didn't have.

When money got tight and we couldn't afford lessons anymore, he trained me for free. Twice a week, every week, for years.

I learned to use nun chucks, do proper katas—pre-arranged patterns of movement designed to simulate real combat—and practice kumite, which are sparring matches used to develop timing, reflexes, and technique.

I earned my black belt at 12 in the art of Taekwondo and Ninjitsu. The test was brutal. Six hours long. Bricks in hand. Endless sparring. Shadowboxing against him. He pushed me to my limit—and then some.

When I passed, it felt like I could do anything. As a registered black belt, I even went to the precinct to register my hands as deadly weapons. That certificate meant everything.

I was invited to fight Ernie Reyes Jr. at Madison Square Garden—a martial artist, actor, and my childhood idol from the movie The Last Dragon. But I wasn't ready. The stage felt too big. The crowd too intimidating. I panicked. My mom said, "If you're not ready, I'll back you." So, I walked away from that match. But I never walked away from what martial arts gave me.

I thanked Sensei Wallace then, and I thank him again now. If you're reading this—thank you. I love you. You saved me.

I watched the movie Fame starring actress Debbie Allen, and said to myself, That's gonna be me. When she delivered that iconic line—"You want fame? Well, fame costs. And right here is where you start paying... in sweat"—I knew she was talking directly to me. From that day forward, Juilliard wasn't just a dream—it became the goal. I saw it as my way out, my ticket to everything beyond Rochdale.

My dream was to attend Juilliard's high school program—the performing arts school that trained some of the greatest talents in the world. No zoning or distance was going to stop me. It was my new dream. And I was going to chase it. But dreams cost money. They also require food in your belly and peace at home—two things we didn't always have.

At 11 years old, I started hustling outside of Key Foods Supermarket, which was located inside what we called "The Big Mall" at Rochdale. It wasn't a traditional mall with big-name department stores, but to us, it was everything—a grocery store, barbershop, pizza spot, and a few other local businesses all under one roof. It was the heart of the community.

Every day, I positioned myself just outside the doors of Key Foods, offering to help people carry their groceries, load their bags into cars, or return their shopping carts. It was a humble hustle, but it meant everything to me. Some people would give me a nickel or a dime. Others handed me a quarter. A few gave me a whole dollar, and every once in a while, someone would give me a five-dollar bill—which felt like I hit the lottery. Other times, all I got was a nod or a polite 'thank you.' They had no idea that those tips were how I ate. No idea that I wasn't just being helpful—I was surviving.

But I kept showing up. Because if I didn't hustle, we didn't eat. While my father laid in bed, I worked. Sunup to Sundown

Some days I made $8, maybe $10. On a good day? $15. That was enough to grab a slice and a soda for myself, plus have enough left over to bring home something small for my mother to cook, or to help her with car fare to get to work. Sometimes that meant a can of salmon or corned beef—whatever we could stretch into a meal. My mom could make a whole dinner out of next to nothing, and I was proud just to bring something home. Every dollar mattered— every hustle helped us survive another day.

That's where I met Boo Boo—aka 50 Cent. He used to box at the "White House," in Rochdale right near the basketball courts and The Mountains. We both had our own hustles. Different grind. Same goal. The "White House" wasn't an actual house—it was a nickname we gave to the building where kids boxed. And "The Mountains" weren't real mountains either—just massive dirt mounds leftover from construction. But to us? They were everything.

Some friends even looked out for me and my moms. One of my neighborhood friends told me straight up, "I didn't sell to her— out of respect for you. But the next person might not feel the same."

And just like that, my secret wasn't a secret anymore. People knew. People knew my parents were on drugs.

And I carried that shame like a second skin. Some nights it was quiet. Too quiet. Other nights it was chaos—slurred arguments, broken promises, empty cabinets. You never knew which version of your parents would show up.

We'd have an egg but no bread. Cereal but no milk. But we always had pecan twirls—leftovers from my dad's short stint at the Hostess factory. That was breakfast, lunch, and dinner. He didn't keep that job long, but while he did, pecan twirls became our staple.

My kids—Jewel, Jayla, and Dante—will never know that life. They've flown on planes, eaten full meals, lived childhoods I only dreamed of. Nas said, "You're wealthy when your kids' upbringing is better than yours." Facts.

I finally got another shot at Julliard—this time for clarinet. I practiced nonstop. Saved money to rent one. My mom's friend V helped cover the rest. I had this old jar I kept on the windowsill labeled "Key Foods" where I'd drop every spare coin I made. That jar was my bank, my hope, my ticket to Juilliard. I'll always be grateful to V for that—she saw my potential even when things were falling apart around us.

The day before my audition, my mom had to work. She asked my father—my father—to take me to Sam Ash to rent it. We got there. He said, "Give me the money, I'll talk them down." I hesitated. He insisted. I gave it to him.

He disappeared. I wasn't just angry—I was shattered. It was the kind of betrayal that sits in your chest and makes it hard to breathe. That audition was supposed to be my way out. And he took that from me. Twenty minutes passed. Then forty. Then over an hour. I walked into the store. They still had the clarinet. No one had seen him.

I begged strangers for change, called my mom on a payphone, and told her what happened. We cried. "Just get home," she said. I hopped the turnstile. When I got to the bus, I told the driver the truth. He saw how distraught and defeated I looked, and out of the kindness of his heart, he let me ride home for free. I came home broken. Angry. Ashamed.

My mom still made me go to the audition. I told Julliard everything. That I had the passion. The hours. The talent. Just not the clarinet. They said, "Sorry. We can't help."

Just like that, the dream was gone again.

Looking back, maybe it had to happen that way. Maybe God was shaping me for something greater. Preparing me for a different kind of stage. One with no script—just legacy.

Even when my dreams got snatched, I never stopped dreaming. And somehow, I kept going. Vanessa was driving us to East Texas, trying to get me to Dante. It felt like forever. But really… we hadn't even made it out of our neighborhood.

CHAPTER 3
"I JUST STABBED HIM..."

The morning Nikita called me and told me they couldn't find Dante, there was this black bird repeatedly slamming into the window of my front door. Over and over, this bird flew into my window. Although I was still half asleep from DJing the club the night before, I remember hearing Vanessa and my mother-in-law talking about the bird, trying to figure out what it wanted and why it couldn't seem to avoid our house. It was slamming into the window like it was trying to tell us something. We would come to understand the message soon after.

Vanessa stopped at a red light on Preston Rd. The duration of a traffic light never seems longer than when you're desperately trying to get somewhere. Looking out the windshield, all I saw was this bright red light, glowing—growing brighter and brighter—yet never changing.

The last time I "saw red" like that, I actually blacked out.

I was 14 years old, in my bedroom watching The Honeymooners. That show was one of my escapes. Something about Ralph Kramden's wild facial expressions, his constant shouting—"One of these days, Alice... POW! Right in the kisser!"—and Ed Norton's goofy timing made me laugh, even when things at home weren't funny. It was old-school, black-and-white, and corny to most, but to me it was comfort. A chance to check out from reality for thirty minutes at a time.

It was around midnight, and my Moms had just gotten in from

her favorite after-work hangout spot, Bentley's. She was a regular there—happy hour was her time to unwind with coworkers, to temporarily escape the chaos of home. My mother was working her ass off, not only to provide for her son but also for her husband. As an adult now, I can understand why she needed that break.

My father, on the other hand, wasn't so understanding. From my bedroom, I could hear all the commotion. The moment she walked through the door, my father—jealous and more than likely high—started antagonizing her. He questioned her in a fit of rage.

Moms wasn't going for the arguing. She told my father she needed to wash off her makeup and proceeded to go into the bathroom, which was adjacent to my room. They kept arguing while she was in there. Growing up in that apartment, I was no stranger to their fights—verbal and physical. The sound of their voices clashing was the background noise of my childhood. My father was emotionally and verbally abusive toward my mother, and she, in return, sometimes let her hands do the talking. But I had never in my life heard my mother scream "STOP!!" the way she did that night.

To be fair, my mother could've very well hit my father first—it wouldn't have been the first time. But I wasn't in the room, so I don't know. What I do know is that her scream told me everything I needed to hear. That scream wasn't from a woman on the offense—it was a cry from someone trying to protect herself.

I jumped up and ran to the bathroom door, banging on it. My father told me to go back to bed, but that wasn't happening. I told him to open the door. Moms called out that she was alright, but I knew better. That "STOP" wasn't the kind of stop someone yells when they're in control. That was a plea. A scream for help.

I snapped. "Open the FUCKING DOOR!"

They kept tussling. I wasn't waiting any longer. All I could think about was everything I learned at the Rochdale Community Center—how to break boards, how to break bricks. So, I stepped back, gathered my power, and kicked the bathroom door off the hinges. The sight on the other side of that door stopped me in my tracks—but only for a second. My superhero needed me.

Her eyeglasses were shattered in the sink. There was a cut above her eyebrow. Blood dripped down her face. And the man standing over her... was the person I had grown to despise. This was the same mother who took me to get stitches when I was five years old. The same woman who worked tirelessly in the city as an administrative assistant to give me a better life. The woman who, despite everything, held it all together.

And now she was crumpled on the bathroom floor, bleeding in her own home. And him? The one hovering above her? That was my father.

The same father who caused those stitches when I was five. The one who stole my Juilliard audition money. The one who dragged my mother into his drug addiction after falling deep into it himself. Hate is a strong word—but at that moment, I hated him with everything in me.

I hated that he brought me into this world only to give me a life like this. I hated the toxic, violent environment he kept us in. I hated what he represented. I hated the damage he was doing to my mother's spirit. The man I hated was hurting my superhero—and at that moment, all I wanted to do was take him out. I blacked out. I mean that literally.

All the years of training from Sensei Robert Wallace came flooding through me like muscle memory. Every pressure point, every strike zone, every move he taught me—I used them. And I used them with everything I had. I went to work on my father. My body was moving faster than my thoughts. I was a machine fueled by rage, trauma, and love for the woman lying on that tile floor. Then I heard it.

"KAREEM!"

My mother's voice—sharp, commanding, full of desperation— snapped me out of the trance. It was as if she pressed pause on the chaos. When I came back to myself, my father was in the bathtub. Bleeding. Limp. A pool of blood beneath him.

Our walls were paper-thin. Somebody must've called the police, because before I knew it, sirens echoed through the building. I walked out of our apartment to a crowd. Everybody in the projects was outside. Police lights. Flashing red and blue. Faces in windows. Mothers holding their kids. The sun coming up had competition that morning.

But nobody expected to see Karate Kareem—the quiet kid who didn't bother nobody—being led to a police car in handcuffs, blood on his shirt, after beating his own father to a pulp. My mother was pleading—first with Rochdale security, then with the police. She was frantic, desperate, trying to save me from a system that wouldn't understand the context.

"Please don't take my baby to jail," she cried.

She even pleaded with my father:

"Tell them not to take him to the precinct!"

But he didn't say a word.

He just stood there—bruised, bleeding, and silent.

This was the same son who just fought him to protect his wife. But instead of speaking up to defend me, he let them take me. Because I was technically the cause of his injuries, the cops had no choice. They had to bring me in. So, there I was, back at the 113th Precinct.

Except this time, I wasn't walking in proudly to register my hands as deadly weapons after earning my black belt. No. This time I was being arrested—for using those same hands to defend my mother. The officers asked my father if he wanted to press charges. I don't remember his response. I just know I was eventually released. So, either he said no, or they decided not to pursue it. But either way, that wasn't the end of it.

It might've been the first time the cops got involved in our family business, but unfortunately... it wouldn't be the last. I was still 14 when I came home from day camp and found out my mother had been arrested. Although she never said it outright, I can imagine what her mindset must've been: "Putting your wife and your son out on the street is not, and never will be, acceptable to me."

My father had taken the rent money and, once again, gone on his so-called "mission"—a term he used to disguise his drug runs. But this time, Moms had enough. She was already mentally checked out of the marriage, but the realization that my father would rather get high than ensure his family had a roof over their heads? That was the final straw. It was my Aunt Linda who told me what happened:

My mother had stabbed my father.

She'd been venting to Aunt Linda about the stolen rent money, and right in the middle of that conversation, my father walked in— more than likely high—with no clue why my mother was upset. That's when all hell broke loose.

Moms hit him first. The fighting started. At some point, my father had her pinned to the floor, his forearm pressing into her neck. In that moment, with no options left, Moms reached for a knife and stabbed him in the arm. She must've hit an artery, because blood sprayed from his arm like a ruptured fire hose—splattering across the walls like an enraged artist painting in crimson. The same walls that heard our arguments now wore the proof of our trauma.

When Moms needed help, and my father wouldn't lift a finger, she turned to my grandfather—James "JT" Thomson. I didn't even know at the time, but he was the one who'd come through with the money to cover the rent.

We didn't have a typical grandfather–grandson relationship, but I knew he loved me. He welcomed me into his home in Brooklyn without hesitation. He wasn't a big talker. He'd point to the kitchen and say there was food if I was hungry, or make me a sandwich, then quietly retreat to his room. But I always knew he was watching over me. And I knew he was looking out for my mother too, even if it wasn't in the most obvious ways.

When he passed, I took leave from the Navy just to attend his funeral. No one expected me to be there, but I showed up. And I buried him with my only set of dog tags—the ones I'd worn during boot camp. I never replaced them. I wanted JT to have a piece of me with him in Heaven.

Moms walked out of the bedroom and calmly told my aunt, "Linda, I just stabbed him. You might want to help him." Shortly after, she was arrested for attempted murder. Since my father didn't die from the stabbing, it felt like déjà vu as I sat, anxiously waiting to see whether he'd press charges. After several days in the hospital, he finally dropped them. And just like that, my mother dropped the marriage. Then, we were homeless.

My Uncle Polcat — my mother's brother — helped us move our belongings out of Rochdale. We didn't have a plan, but we had no choice. Our next stop was a rundown hotel. The bedbugs must've checked in before we did.

I remember waking up covered in red bumps from being bitten in my sleep. The discomfort was intense, but the worst part wasn't the itching — it was watching my mother do everything she could to make sure I was comfortable, even in a place that didn't feel safe or clean. That's what stood out the most. Just like when I needed stitches at five years old, she showed up for me. She always showed up. But we couldn't stay there long. It wasn't livable.

My godmother, whom I affectionately call Aunt Maggie, lived just one building over from our old apartment in Rochdale. She and her husband, along with their son and daughter, shared a two-bedroom. Even in those tight quarters, Aunt Maggie made space. She gave me her couch, and I laid my head there for what felt like forever.

Eventually, the weight of the situation became too heavy for everyone. The space was overcrowded, tensions were high, and my extended stay was taking a toll on the household. But I'll never forget what she did for us. To this day, I'm grateful for Aunt Maggie — for her heart, her home, and the grace she extended during one of the darkest chapters of our lives.

I looked over at Vanessa, still stuck at that red light on Preston Rd., and I couldn't help but reflect. I couldn't imagine her eyeglasses shattered in the bathroom sink. I couldn't imagine her face bloodied, bruised, or swollen. I couldn't imagine telling my son to go back to sleep while standing over the woman I love, the way my father had done to me and my mother.

In fact, one of the things Vanessa and I argued about the most was my approach to fixing things with Dante — especially when it came to him accepting her. Looking back, I understand his perspective more clearly. But at the time, the stubborn Taurus in me thought, "If she makes me happy, why can't you just be happy for me?"

What I failed to ask myself was: how did Dante feel?

How did he feel watching his father marry a woman who wasn't his mom? How did he feel when I expected him to just be okay with it, without even considering his side of things? I didn't take the time to understand the conflict within him. Vanessa challenged me on that — and I thank God she did. She helped me see what I couldn't see on my own. She taught me how to be a better father, a better man, and a better husband.

We came from two different worlds. I grew up in the projects with a working mother who carried the weight of a household and a husband addicted to drugs. Vanessa came from a two-parent home with a backyard and a mortgage. She never had to hustle outside Key Food just to eat. She didn't know the feeling of looking in an empty refrigerator and already knowing there wouldn't be another paycheck for two weeks. Her dad didn't take money meant for something important and disappear. She didn't grow up hating her father.

So sometimes, I felt like she couldn't possibly understand me. And when we'd argue, I'd weaponize that difference — her stability

— as if her lack of struggle invalidated her insight. But I've grown. I now realize that because Vanessa came from something different, she had something valuable to offer. She knew what a stable home looked like. She had an example of a husband who led and loved his family. She knew what consistency felt like.

In our home growing up, my mother played the role of both parents. She made everything happen. She held it down. As a child, I'm sure she had to drag my father along just to participate in anything that resembled family unity. And in the early years of my marriage, Vanessa had to do the same with me.

I didn't realize how important family time was because I never had it. I was too busy surviving to appreciate things like game nights, dinners, or vacations. But over time, Vanessa helped me change that. She helped me repair what was broken between me and Dante. She helped shape how I father my daughters, Jewel and Jayla. She helped me show up, not just physically, but emotionally — for the little things, the important things, and everything in between. Family trips. Dinner conversations. Sunday rest. That's all Vanessa Rose.

The light on Preston finally turned green, and Vanessa pressed the gas. We were on our way to find my son.

CHAPTER 4
"THE KITCHEN IS CLOSED..."

I worked extremely hard for my family. At times, maybe too hard.

Chasing the bag to make sure my family never knew what it felt like to starve—that was my way of paying my mother back for every sacrifice she made for me. Not just the financial sacrifices. I'm talking about the trauma she endured at the hands of my father, the guilt of falling into addiction while trying to raise a child, and the constant uncertainty of everyday life in New York City. I wanted not only my family—but especially my Moms—to know I would always grind to make sure they never needed for anything.

Tupac wrote one of the most relatable pieces of music with "Dear Mama."

I'd like to think most of us from the hood can feel those lyrics, especially when Pac said, "Mama made miracles every Thanksgiving." That hit me on a deeper level than most. There were days we had absolutely nothing in the fridge. But somehow, on holidays, my mother would come through. She made those dinners stretch—and they're still etched into my memory.

I'll never forget one Thanksgiving before my father caused us to get evicted from Rochdale. My mother was coming home from work in Manhattan. She'd already bought everything we needed for dinner—she was pulling off another miracle. But before she could make it home, she was stripped of everything: her safety, her stability, and her ability to provide.

Some piece of shit shoved my mother into a telephone booth and robbed her. He took her money. He even took the food she had just bought for Thanksgiving. Did this heartless bastard know how hard my mother worked just to make that meal happen? Did he care that there were days I gave her my own money just so she could ride the subway to work?

If I'd been there, things might've gone differently. But he didn't know—and he damn sure didn't care. That's what New York was like. Everybody trying to survive. Eat or be eaten. At least my Moms and I were doing it legally. There was a point in time when I ain't even like Thanksgiving because of that incident. Why would I care about a day that reminded me of when my superhero got robbed?

I have so many trauma triggers—it's part of why it took Vanessa so long to help me understand the importance of quality time during holidays like Thanksgiving. And trust me, wifey throws down. Her Thanksgiving dinners are legendary. Growing up, we had Cornish hens with rice and maybe some sweet corn. Now? We've upgraded to Cajun turkey, baked mac and cheese, candied yams—all the classics.

But Vanessa's curry chicken? That's my kryptonite. If I'm on a diet or in workout mode and she makes curry chicken? It's a wrap. I'm folding. Funny enough, it was my cooking that got her at first.

On our first adult date, I cooked for her—rib tips, rice, spinach…something light but solid. She was impressed. What she didn't know at the time? Those rib tips came out the box. The rice was instant. The spinach was straight out the freezer. She still tells people I "swindled" her into thinking I could cook. And I guess she's right. But hey—it worked.

My daughters, Jewel and Jayla? They love crab legs and lobster. Imagine being under 18 with a palate for delicacies. Dante once tried to put me on to quail—but I couldn't do it. That bird just looked too weird. What he did put me on to was Ocean Water from Sonic. That became our thing.

Maybe I did overdo it with the clubs. Maybe I worked too many nights and missed too many milestones. But I did it to make sure my girls could eat well and live better. I did it so my son could casually put me on to fast food drinks that, at his age, I could've never even afforded. But with time, you realize—nothing is more valuable than time. You can chase the bag all day long, but you can't buy back the moments you miss.

Speaking of time, the minutes felt like hours as we raced to East Texas to see about Dante. Vanessa and I had taken this drive every Christmas to see him. Every year, I'd make sure he got anything and everything he wanted.

See, as a long-distance father, sometimes you try to compensate for your absence with gifts. You hope that by buying them things, you can make up for the moments you missed. That the shoes or game consoles or cash can cover the gaps in time. I know it's not ideal, but it's real. And I always wanted to see that joy on my son's face.

The same joy I felt that Christmas when I was seven years old and got a New York Giants–blue mountain bike…before it got stolen. So yeah—I chased the bag, hard. For them. For that joy. At the time, my grind was paying off. I had a ten-year residency at one of the hottest clubs in Dallas—Park Ave. I had spun live on BET's 106 & Park and even on Revolt TV. That night before Nikita called me? I'd just rocked Park Ave. again.

But now? None of those accolades meant a damn thing. What difference did any of it make if I didn't know where my son was? Was it worth missing key moments in Dante's life just to make a name for myself? Yes, we spoke every day, and yes, we saw each other often—but could it have been more? Should it have been more?

Let me tell you something real: That bag don't mean shit when it comes to your child. You can't spend success to buy back time. I loved my mother deeply for doing her best to provide after we left my father. But when we escaped that bedbug-infested hotel, she couldn't care for me full-time.

So, she reached out to her sister in Flushing, Queens, and asked if I could stay there "for a while." What was supposed to be temporary turned into a sleepover with no expiration date... and no one acknowledging the truth of what I was going through. Pomonok Apartments, however, were lacking in size.

This small two-bedroom apartment was home to my aunt and her three children, my cousins. They filled the bedrooms, so I made a pallet on the living room floor. But I was used to that. I'd slept on floors before—so traumatized, I probably could've slept standing up.

I was grateful to have a roof over my head and no more bedbug bites... but that didn't change the fact that I was essentially homeless. And worse—separated from my mother. My moms never abandoned me. Never. She wasn't somewhere smoking up my dreams like my father. Her decision came from a place of sacrifice. She thought she was doing what was best for me, even if it meant we couldn't be together.

But that didn't make it easier. The woman who'd always been there—my superhero—was now somewhere else. And I wasn't on the Southside anymore. Now, when I left for school, I went in the opposite direction. And the same floors where our family used to party and dance were now the floors I slept on. Except for the weekends.

On Fridays, I was gone—back to Rochdale. Any holiday, any 4-day weekend, I was home. My real home. I never felt comfortable in Flushing, and it wasn't because of my aunt. It just wasn't the Southside. And I needed to be back where my heart was.

My mother was staying with an older gentleman named PooPoo. I didn't know what their arrangement was. I didn't care. All I knew was that I wanted to see her. I'd visit her and crash at a friend's house. Randy Parker—who would later be known in the industry as ES$O—lived in Building #9, Circle 3 in Rochdale. My boy Dwight Parham, aka Bunkin, was in the same building. Those two? My brothers.

We'd been tight since we were around ten or eleven, running ball together nonstop. They let me borrow clothes so I wouldn't wear the same outfit three days in a row. They'd give me a few dollars for food without hesitation. Because that's what family does. And to this day, they still are my family. Just because you are blood doesn't mean you are family.

I have plenty of relatives, but the truth is—"family" is a title you earn. Relatives might share your DNA, but that doesn't mean they rock with you. They may not support you, may not have your best interests at heart.

Family? Family would give you the shirt off their back without a second thought. Family checks in on you. Family opens their door without asking for anything in return—except maybe that you keep your head up and keep pushing. If they had a dollar, you had fifty cents.

And some so-called family? You can't even call them for a single dollar. So yeah—I'm cautious with who I give my energy to. I protect my peace. Because when you've been through what I've been through, you have no choice but to keep your circle solid and small. I don't know if my approach is right or wrong, but it's necessary. It's how I stay mentally, physically, and emotionally stable.

If it wasn't for the people who stepped up for me in high school, I would've been even hungrier—literally and emotionally. Vanessa. Bunkin. My real ones. They came through when I needed them the most. They paid for lunch. Bought me chocolate cookies just to get me through the day.

My Geometry teacher, Ms. Knors? She stayed stocked with butter cookies and fudge cookies—the ones that came two in a pack. I'll never forget her. She was one of the good ones. One of those teachers who truly saw her students. She gave us space when we needed it. We'd hang out in her office when we probably should've been in class. She'd fuss at us a little but never kick us out. She didn't ask too many questions—maybe because she knew sometimes school was more about survival than grades.

And for me, those cookies were sometimes the only thing I'd eat all day. I was on an empty stomach as my wife and I raced to East Texas to get to my son. But the feeling in the pit of my stomach wasn't from hunger—it was fear. It was dread. It was every unanswered question crashing into me all at once.

Why hasn't Nikita called me back yet?

How long has it been?

Why isn't anybody updating me on my son?

Logically, I knew if Nikita had an update, I'd hear it too. But when your heart is in full-blown panic mode, logic takes a back seat. It's like your body's present, but your mind is racing faster than the car you're riding in. As we passed a Kroger's, I couldn't help but think back to those days I hustled outside Key Foods just trying to make it. Trying to survive.

There were times I was out there in the cold, trying to scrape up enough change to buy a can of salmon so we could eat. Trying to earn car fare for my Moms so she could make it to work in the city. That kind of hunger? That kind of drive? It stays with you.

It doesn't matter how far you go in life—you remember. You remember the look on your mother's face when she's counting coins just to get on the train. You remember what it feels like to have nothing—and vow to never let your kids experience that.

As long as I had breath in my body, my children would never know what it felt like to stand outside a grocery store hoping to make enough money to eat that night. Never. Dante was still in high school and already getting paid DJ gigs. My daughters? They out here eating crab legs and lobster like it's nothing. They're not hustling for dinner—they're ordering DoorDash with extra sauce.

That's what all those missed meals and sleepless nights were for. That was my why. But in that moment—none of that mattered. Not the money. Not the gigs. Not the flashy life. All I could think about was whether my son was okay.

My days hustling outside of Key Foods were over once I left Rochdale. But my hunger? That never left me. I just channeled it into something different. I traded my Karate Gi for a basketball jersey—number 15.

I became the point guard for the Jamaica Beavers, while Bunkin—my brother from another—held down the 2-guard spot in number 25. And I was nice. I wasn't just playing to play—I was out there cooking. I made it into elite camps, went head-to-head with future NBA legends like Stephon Marbury and Kenny Anderson before they shook David Stern's hand on draft night.

My favorite point guard? Mark "Action" Jackson. Queens-born, St. John's baller, NY Knicks floor general—just like me, he made it from the city's grind to the big lights. But while he was running plays in the Garden, I was balling for bread. No million-dollar contract, no ESPN coverage—just raw talent and a growling stomach.

And while we were out there getting buckets, guess who else was making plays? Boo Boo—aka Curtis "50 Cent" Jackson. He wasn't rapping yet. Back then, 50 was holding it down at the courts with a dice game called Cee-lo.

It was the game of the hood—three dice, cold pavement, and a whole lot of risk. And 50? He always had the bank. He controlled the table. He was the one everybody was watching—even while they watched us hoop. He and the other hustlers used to place side bets on the games.

"Yo, I got ten on Kareem dropping 15."

I'd hear it as I laced up my kicks. Pressure? Maybe. But I delivered—empty stomach and all. It's a wild feeling when people can literally hear your stomach growl while you're dropping dimes and hitting jumpers. You lock in, zone out... until the final whistle blows. Then the silence of your own reality creeps back in: You still don't know if you'll eat that night.

And that day I'll never forget—the day I learned the real difference between family and relatives.

My aunt in Flushing had a 7:00 PM curfew rule. Usually, I was back in time without a problem. But on this day—maybe practice ran late, maybe I just needed to breathe—I was about 15 minutes behind schedule. And I was starving. No lunch. No butter cookies. No after-school snacks from Ms. Knors. Just straight hunger pains that made my whole body feel weak.

I got to the door. She opened it. Just a few steps in was the kitchen. And all I wanted—needed—was a plate of food. I was drained, but I tried to speak up respectfully. "Auntie... can I eat something?" She didn't even hesitate.

"You're late. The kitchen is closed."

What?

I stood there frozen. Did she really just say that? I'm 14 years old. I live here. I'm your sister's son. And I'm hungry as hell. "I haven't eaten all day," I pleaded. "Auntie, please..." She stood firm, cold with it: "That's not my problem. The kitchen is closed." I didn't know whether to be angry or embarrassed.

Her kitchen was the size of a damn closet, but in that moment, it might as well have been a locked vault. She was denying me basic survival. So, I did what I had to do. I picked up the house phone and called my Moms.

I told her straight up: "Auntie said the kitchen is closed. She won't let me eat." That phone call revealed something I wasn't ready to hear. In the heat of their argument, I overheard that my mother had been paying her own sister $75 to $100 a week just so I could sleep on a pallet on her floor. But Moms had missed a payment that week...and now her sister—my aunt—was making me pay for it.

I didn't say much else. I walked out. Tears streamed down my face on the way to the bodega to pick up the money my Moms had wired me through Western Union. I wasn't just crying from hunger. I was crying from humiliation. From betrayal. From pain that had nowhere else to go.

My father put us in this situation. My mother was doing her best to clean it up. And here I was… just a kid caught in the middle, wondering: Why the fuck do I have to go through this? Why me?! Looking back, maybe my aunt had her reasons. Maybe that money was for groceries.Maybe she was struggling too.

But when you tell a kid—your blood—that he can't eat because his mom missed a payment…You don't just close the kitchen. You close the door to trust. And after that night, I never felt welcome in her home again. Within a week, after a conversation between Moms and the man she was staying with, I was back in Rochdale. Back on the Southside.

Back with the one person who, even in her own brokenness, never stopped trying to feed me—body and soul. That reunion meant everything. Just like the one I was praying for as Vanessa and I kept driving—racing—to reach my son.

I was finally back on the Southside, sleeping under the same roof as my Moms again. That alone gave me strength—just knowing I was in the one place that had always felt like home. Even if we didn't have much, we had us. And that meant everything.

As Vanessa and I continued racing toward East Texas, that same need to return to my son was all I could feel. I had no idea what condition he was in. No answers. No updates. Just a sick pit in my stomach and a mind that couldn't stop replaying worst-case scenarios.

That drive…Every road sign…Every red light…Every second of silence…It all felt like forever. I couldn't stop thinking about the sacrifices I'd made—working all those late nights at the club, taking extra bookings, chasing that damn bag. I told myself I was doing it for them. For Dante. For Jewel. For Jayla. For Vanessa. For Moms. But in that moment, none of it mattered.

All I wanted was time. Time to hold my son. Time to tell him I loved him. Time to show him that all the missed games, missed phone calls, missed holidays—it wasn't because I didn't care. It was because I was trying to provide.

But the truth is...You can never buy back time. Not with a paycheck. Not with a new pair of Jordans. Not with crab legs or lobster tails. Not even with love—if that love isn't present. I learned that the hard way. I've lived it. And that's why this chapter in my life... this journey to reach Dante... felt like more than just a physical drive.

It was spiritual. It was emotional. It was necessary. Because the kitchen might've been closed back then...But now, as a man, a father, and a husband...I stay open. Open to growth. Open to healing. Open to forgiveness. Open to being present—for real this time.

And God willing, I'd make it in time to open my arms for my son... one more time.

CHAPTER 5
"I'M DOING THIS FOR US..."

Besides Dante's grandfather — Nikita's father — I was the only father figure Dante had ever known. And I figured if I could just keep my promise to be nothing like my own father, then my children would have a dad they could be proud of.

My bonus son, Jawaun — Vanessa's first child — has a great relationship with his own father, and he and I are close as well. Imagine having not one, but two father figures in your life. I'm grateful I've been able to help guide his journey and offer the kind of support I never knew from my own dad.

I still remember meeting Vanessa's father for the first time. I was just her high school boyfriend then, but I was also the first boy she ever brought home. So, it was special — for her and for us. We were having a family reunion at my uncle's house in Long Island, and before Vanessa could come, I had to meet her parents. Her father was no joke. He gave me the same look I'm sure I'll be giving the boys who try to come around my daughters — many, many years from now.

Pops made it very clear: Have her back on time. Make sure my daughter is safe. I'm not playing no games with you. Raymond Rose was the truth, and I respected him for being something I'd never really experienced — a caring, involved father.

If I didn't respect my biological father, there was no way another man would just step in and assume some kind of authority over me. So, while PooPoo — the man with whom my mother and I were staying — was cool, his apartment didn't exactly feel like home. It was just a roof over my head, and I was back with my mother. Nothing more, nothing less.

I was comfortable being back in familiar territory, so returning to Rochdale gave me a little peace. But as I lay on yet another pallet on the floor, I still felt homeless. Technically, I was. PooPoo's apartment definitely wasn't home. Even as a 10th grader, I knew Moms couldn't have been in love with this man. My mother had flavor — and PooPoo did not.

No disrespect to him — he was a nice guy — but he was in his late 60s or early 70s. He talked "old" and dressed "old." God willing, I'll make it to that age myself, but as a 15-year-old, the last thing I wanted to see was a senior citizen walking around the house in a wife-beater or t-shirt and some saggy-ass draws. That was basically his uniform — his version of pajamas, if you will. Moms must've liked him a little, but I always felt she only cared enough to stay there while she worked on getting back on her feet.

I didn't want to go to PooPoo's house after leaving my aunt in Flushing. Of course, I wanted to be back with my superhero — and I was happy to once again be walking distance from Randy and Bunkin. I was walking distance from the big mall, from the Key Food I used to hustle in front of, just trying to make enough money to eat. It was traumatizing territory, but it was also familiar. Southside Jamaica Queens was — and still is — my comfort zone.

But I was ready for us to have our own. I was praying that sooner or later, me and my Moms would be back on our feet and doing our own thing — not having to depend on anybody. I was ready for God's blessing. I was praying to finally break free of the cycle of feeling unwanted, feeling unwelcomed.

My being there seemed to cause a little friction. PooPoo had a younger brother, Horace, and while he was never outright rude to me, I could tell he had issues with a teenager in the house. Horace was younger than PooPoo, but still "old" — definitely in his 60s. And even though it was PooPoo who paid the biggest share of the bills and had the final say, my presence once again stirred up tension between siblings — like I had a choice in where I lived.

At least PooPoo let me eat. Actually, he cooked often and wasn't bad at it. That might've been one of the things that drew my mother to him. I didn't always agree with what he cooked — but it was his house, and if I wanted to eat, I had to eat what was served.

One time, he made pig feet with rice and lima beans. I didn't really eat pork — other than bacon — and I damn sure had never seen a pig's foot on a plate before. All I kept thinking was, what the hell am I eating? I did talk to him about it, but there was no negotiation. If you were hungry, you either ate what was made, or you went without.

Honestly, pig feet look ugly as hell. But surprisingly, they didn't taste all that bad. Still wasn't my thing though. I was too grossed out to care what it tasted like. All I could think was: Why the hell am I eating the foot of a pig? The answer, unfortunately, was the same reason I'd end up putting hands on PooPoo later: I didn't have a choice.

I wanted my mother to have peace of mind. She deserved to have some kind of room to breathe and just be a person — not my mom, not my superhero. Just herself. She deserved to hang out, have fun, and live her life. And though I yearned for a better situation for us, I also knew my presence must've put pressure on her to provide it. Who was I to be selfish and not want to see her happy?

Well… like my father a few months earlier, PooPoo didn't appreciate my mother coming back to his house "late." I don't know if he thought he could enforce a curfew on a grown woman, but it was his house, and he had his rules. And one of those rules included a time to be in the crib.

Moms was usually home by 7 or 7:30. But on this particular night, she got to PooPoo's place around 8:30or 9. She had obviously gone out after work. But now she wasn't being allowed into the home where she lived.

She had a key, but he had double-locked the door, meaning he had to unlock it from the inside. From my pallet on the living room floor, I heard her knocking, then her voice. But PooPoo was standing there at the door, antagonizing her. It was like he got a kick out of it.

I asked him straight up: "You not gone let my mother in?"

Either Moms was coming in, or I was going out. But either way, nobody was separating me from my mother again.

He was talking to her through the peephole like she was a stranger. But Moms wasn't having it. I heard her say, "You got my son in there — you gone let me in this house." Damn right, Moms.

Eventually, he did. But that didn't stop the argument. They took it into the bedroom, and the arguing just kept going. By now, I wasn't even fazed — I was used to loud disagreements that could get physical real quick. But I was always on standby. If she needed me, I'd be ready.

I remember thinking: This isn't even my father. Yet here we are again, forced to live in a less-than-ideal situation, just trying to survive it. I wasn't hustling outside of Key Food anymore, and whatever money I made playing on the basketball courts wasn't nearly enough. Our situation was so damn frustrating, and I knew for a fact that I could've hit up Boo Boo — a.k.a. 50 Cent — and asked for a pack to move on the streets. I could've made us enough money in two days to get out of PooPoo's house.

But knowing what that shit had done to my father — and what it did to my Moms — I couldn't bring myself to sell poison to somebody else's parents. How could I destroy the same community that was already destroying me?

And that's no knock to 50 or anyone who did what they had to do to survive. We all make choices based on our circumstances. And believe me, I understood the temptation of easy money.

On "Hate It or Love It," 50 rapped:

"I wanna live good, so shit, I sell dope."

I wanted to live good too — so who was I to judge?

But with all the chances I had to go left, something — maybe

God — kept pulling me right.

J. Cole, who's talked about watching his mother battle drug addiction, said it best on "Breakdown":

"You made a milli off of selling hard white? Yeah right.

My mama tell you what addicted to that pipe feel like?"

Then it happened.

When I heard Moms yell —

"KAREEM!" —

I knew my superhero was in trouble.

It took me no time. I shot up from my pallet, ran past the kitchen, through the hallway, and straight toward PooPoo's bedroom. And unlike the situation with my father, I wasn't knocking. I wasn't asking. I wasn't hesitating.

With every ounce of my strength, I launched a full-force karate kick and knocked that door clean off the hinges.

It felt like I ran straight through the damn door. And once I crossed that threshold, I saw a scene I was too familiar with: a man tussling with my mother.

I didn't wait. I went straight into attack mode.

I put PooPoo in a clean little chokehold — just enough to restrain him and calm him down. He didn't fight back. There was no fighting me back — not when I was protecting my Moms.

Then I heard it again —

"KAREEM!" —

and just like that, my brain got the signal: Fall back. My mother was okay now.

Horace's room was right next to PooPoo's, so naturally, he came running when he heard the commotion. PooPoo wasn't bloody, but he was definitely bruised up. Once he got his wind and his composure back, he said:

"Y'all gotta get the fuck out my house!"

He didn't make us leave that night, but he did kick my mother out of the bedroom. She had to sleep beside me on a pallet on the floor.

And yet again, my mother didn't fold. She was a hustler — it's where I get it from. Unbeknownst to me, she already had money saved and was working on a plan to get us out of there.

I'm guessing she had a conversation with PooPoo and asked for a little more time. Either way, within a few days, we were gone. She made it happen. Just like always. My superhero came through.

We moved into Ms. Connor's house — a three-family home on 175th Street and Jamaica Avenue in Queens. There was a family living in the basement, Ms. Connor lived in the middle, and Moms and I moved upstairs.

That 2-bedroom apartment couldn't have been more than 700 square feet — but it was ours. Not PooPoo's. Not a borrowed living room floor. Not a situation where my presence was barely tolerated. It was our space. Our restart.

I had my own room again. With a bed. Moms had her own room. We shared a bathroom, but there would never again be a night when I'd hear her yell for help behind a locked door. There'd never again be a morning where her blood or broken glasses would be in the sink. Never again.

The kitchen was small — so small you could barely cook and stand in it at the same time — but it was open. The living room was tiny — barely fit a couch, loveseat, and TV — but I would never again have to make a pallet on that floor. I was proud of Moms.

She was no longer under the influence of my father or any man. She worked hard. She fought tooth and nail. And she got us back on our feet — together — on our own terms.

I was proud to walk through the gate at Ms. Connor's house, through that little front yard, up those stairs, and into our apartment.

Our apartment.

Everything was falling into place at home… then my relationship with Vanessa fell apart.

Young and dumb — that was me. I cheated on her. Not because I didn't love her, not because I was looking for something better, but simply because I was a kid and didn't realize what I had.

I was beatboxing on the cafeteria table — the girl started dancing to my beat — and that was enough for me to blow up everything I had with Vanessa. The girl I cheated with would become my girlfriend immediately after. She was a cheerleader like Vanessa, just a year younger.

Vanessa's cut-off game? Elite. I tried to get her back. My boys, Toine and Bunkin, even tried to smooth things over — but she wasn't having it. At all.

I was her first. We were in love. And I stepped out on her over nothing — just curiosity. While she wasn't my first, it felt like she was, because it actually meant something. The connection, the chemistry, the depth of emotion — everything between us was real. It wasn't just physical; it was personal. We were teenagers, but when we "did it," it was a manifestation of what we felt.

That experience between us? Unforgettable.

I still joke with my wife about it to this day.

After we broke up, Vanessa started dating a basketball player who was a year older than us. So now, not only am I seeing her cheering while I'm playing, but she wouldn't even look in my direction during school. It was brutal.

Back then, I didn't give the breakup much thought. But by senior year? I missed my friend. I missed talking to her. I missed her presence. I missed playing spades at Randy's house in Rochdale. I missed walking through Green Acres Mall with her. I just missed her. The longing for Vanessa didn't go away. It followed me into adulthood.

By the time I hit my twenties, I told myself: If I ever find that woman again, I'm going to marry her.

Bunkin used to joke, "Man, what if she's 300 pounds now?"

"I'ma just put her on a diet!"

I didn't care. I knew who I wanted. I knew who I needed. Vanessa Rose is the only woman I've ever loved unconditionally. We wouldn't cross paths or speak again for 16 years. But as high school seniors, we had both moved on.

Mom and I walked to my high school graduation. My royal blue cap and gown marked the end of one chapter and the beginning of a new journey.

I was voted Best Looking, Best Dancer, and Most Sexy. But you won't find a picture of me next to any of those accomplishments in the yearbook. There's only one picture — I was also voted Mr. Attitude, and the mean mug on my face says it all.

I was actually present for picture day... I just didn't take the pictures. I hated pictures. I didn't want anyone to look through my eyes and into my soul. If you really saw me, then you'd see everything. You'd see the pain. You'd see the rage. And I didn't want to be seen.

I was popular — but I didn't want to be popular.

Speaking of pictures, I used to joke that after graduation I wanted to represent everybody who ever had a mugshot — because I was planning to become a criminal defense attorney. That was the goal.

I enrolled at John Jay University and majored in law. My basketball career was short-lived there, and honestly, so was my time at college altogether. I flunked out after about a year.

But I did enjoy Psych 101 and 102. The professor was Dr. Jeff Gardere — a well-known celebrity psychologist who would later be a guest on the morning radio show I produced in Dallas. We'll get to that later. Dr. Jeff eventually became known as "America's Psychologist" — and rightfully so.

I'm pretty sure I failed out of college because his was the only class I went to.

Now here I was, no degree… no basketball… no plan.

We were broke. Really broke.

White Castle used to have this deal — 20 plain burgers, fries, and a drink for ten bucks. Me, Bunkin, and Randy would go in on it and split everything.

We called those little sliders "murder burgers" — because they'd murder your stomach and have you running to the toilet. But it's what we could afford. Broke as hell… and still trying to figure out what was next.

I did learn how to drive, though. After getting a credit card in college, I figured out how to rent cars without showing ID — and that's how I taught myself to drive on the streets of New York.

Didn't do me much good without actually owning a car, but still — it was a step.

Me and Bunkin definitely needed money, but we weren't trying to work long-term jobs. So we'd rotate — take turns working for two weeks, then quit and support the other one until it was his turn again. That was the system.

And we worked everywhere:

A&S (which later became Macy's), UPS, a women's clothing store, even a foot messenger job — delivering packages all around Manhattan by foot. That messenger job was the only one I actually held down longer than a few weeks.

We even tried construction once. Didn't make it past orientation.

Here's how that went:

A few Southside hustlers who were on probation told us about construction jobs they worked while trying to stay out of jail. One of them set up a "meeting" for us to get hired.

Turns out, the meeting was just a street dude giving a speech. And about an hour into it, we realized these guys were forcing companies to hire them — like, literally 30-deep, pulling up and intimidating site managers. If the company said no, they got beat down.

The guy giving the speech even admitted,

"I lost some teeth yesterday — but we got him on! Niggas don't understand, we gone get on!"

He was missing teeth.

Me and Bunkin? We hopped on that bus so fast and went right back to Rochdale. That life wasn't for us.

But truthfully… I was still at a loss.

I didn't know what I was going to do with my life.

Then one day, I was walking down Jamaica Avenue by the Coliseum — a legendary hangout spot in Queens. That place was filled with firsts: first fight, first girl, first 3-finger ring. I even got my first gold fronts and pager there.

On that day, I had barely scraped together enough money for some McDonald's. I was eating McNuggets when a Navy recruiter approached me. Clean cut. Young. You could tell he had a good read on people.

I think he saw something in me — a tired young man who just needed structure. He saw I had potential, just no direction.

He asked,

"What are you doing with your life?"

"Man, I don't know. Working odd jobs. Trying to figure it out."

"What about school?"

"I flunked out. Not really sure school's for me either."

What I did know was that I needed discipline.

The same kind of structure Sensei Robert Wallace gave me when I was seven years old — I needed it again now, at nineteen.

The recruiter started selling me the dream:

"You can travel the world. Go to school for free. Build a real career."

At that point, the only part of the world I'd seen outside New York was Freaknik in Atlanta — wild parties, concerts, and half-naked women. It was fun, but I knew there was more out there than just Georgia and the five boroughs.

So I signed up.

Scheduled my MEPS test. Took my physical. I was in.

Convincing Bunkin was easy. We were Frick and Frack, broke and broker.

"Bro, what else are you doing? Might as well come with me."

He bought into the same dream the recruiter sold me.

Moms wasn't happy.

"No, the fuck you ain't!" she snapped when I told her I was joining the Navy.

But I was 19. I told her I was an adult and this was my decision.

It crushed me when she cried.

"So, you don't wanna be here with me no more?" she asked.

She didn't understand at the time — but I get it now. As a father,

I completely understand.

She was scared.

But I had to go.

Living under my mother's roof had become a crutch.

I wasn't a mama's boy, but I also wasn't going to become a man while still in her house.

So, I looked her in the eyes and said:

"Mommy, I'm doing this for us. I love you, and I'm doing this so I can ultimately take care of you. I'm gonna make sure you retire, because I don't want you to have to work all your life. Let me become a man — because this man is going to be the one who retires you.

Unlike my father, this man is gonna be the one who takes care of you."

And while that man was gearing up for boot camp, he and his wife were driving down the Dallas North Tollway...

...one step closer to East Texas, to see about taking care of his son, Dante.

CHAPTER 6
"I'M REALLY A FATHER…"

Wifey and I had maybe two hours left before we got to East Texas to see about Dante. But the way she was driving, it definitely wouldn't take that long. As frantic as we both were, deep down I was holding on to the belief that my son was okay. He's an excellent swimmer, and it was April in Texas—it's not like the lake was frozen. This was ideal weather to be outside. Soon we'd be there, and everything would have to be okay.

Speaking of frozen lakes, a 19-year-old Kareem Thomson was now a military recruit doing his time in basic training in Great Lakes, Illinois, just north of Chicago. And it was cold as hell. I'm from New York. New York is brick cold. But Great Lakes? That's brick cold times ten. And it was December.

The temperature didn't concern our superiors at all. For ten weeks, we marched outside every day. Physical training, or PT—we marched outside. To get chow—we marched outside. Every day we fell into single-file formation, marching to that same "1, 2, 3, 4" cadence you've probably seen in every military movie or TV show.

When I say it was cold, I mean unbelievably frigid. The naval base sat right on Lake Michigan—hence the name. I remember one day it was -30 degrees outside. Dead serious. Our Company Commander gave us the option: march to chow or stay in the barracks. Some brave souls decided to go. I was one of them.

See, once you've known what it feels like to go without food, you'll never choose to starve. I wasn't about to skip a meal. And we weren't marching for no damn butter cookies. Our meals were decent—hot dogs, burgers, baked chicken, rice. Better than the McNuggets I had the day I enlisted. They only gave us ten minutes to eat, but at least they fed us.

So, I threw on everything I had—uniform, pea coat, face mask, beanie—layered up like a soldier and made that march. It was so cold, your spit would freeze in midair when you talked. No exaggeration. But I'm from Southside Jamaica Queens. The cold wasn't enough to make me fold. My life had already been cold enough.

Boot camp was basically a hazing process, to say the least. But what can you do to a teenager who's already lived through more pain than most people experience in a lifetime?

I'd already been homeless. I knew what it was like to go days without food. I'd had my best Christmas gift stolen just days after unwrapping it. I watched my father steal the money meant for the clarinet that was supposed to be my golden ticket out of poverty. I knew what it felt like to be denied a plate of food by people who knew I hadn't eaten that day. I'd had to fight my own father for putting his hands on my mother. I witnessed addiction take the man my mother loved and turn him into someone we barely recognized.

I'd already survived some of my darkest moments.

So yeah—boot camp was hard, but it wasn't going to break me.

If I stayed in New York, I would've rotted. I knew it. I would've ended up bitter, stuck, or worse. Once I decided that the Navy was my only way out, there was no looking back. This was my shot at something better. I wasn't going to let anyone take that away from me—not with words, not with cold, not with pain. I was determined to make something of myself. I was already forged in fire. I wasn't about to fold now.

Some others weren't so lucky.

There was this kid named Jamal from Brooklyn. You could tell life had been hard for him. He had that same New York edge—like he'd already had to fight for everything. Jamal had a chip on his shoulder, and the Company Commanders smelled it. They could sense when someone came from the streets, when someone had something to prove. And once they sniffed that out, they went full attack mode: extra PT, constant berating, trying to wear you down physically and mentally. And they broke him.

Jamal cracked under the pressure. Not because he was weak, but because life had already worn him thin.

It reminded me of that scene in Boyz n the Hood. Remember Tre? The strait-laced kid trying to do right—but the streets didn't care. Even with a good father, even with guidance, Tre still broke down. His best friend got murdered. The cops harassed him for simply existing. All that trauma boiled over, and he just started swinging at the air, fists flying at nothing, just trying to let it out.

Jamal was like Tre—fed up, exhausted, and drowning in frustration. And I understood him more than I wanted to admit.

But me? I wasn't breaking.

Bunkin and I were still standing tall. That was my brother. We'd enlisted together, trained together, endured the same freezing cold together. We hooped every day before we joined the Navy, so PT was nothing to us. We made a silent pact that no matter what they threw at us, we wouldn't let each other fall. That bond made all the difference.

I did miss my moms, though.

We were only allowed to call home on holidays, so the only thing we really looked forward to was mail call. That moment when the drill instructor shouted your name and handed you a letter—it meant the world. It wasn't just paper. It was connection. It was warmth. It was a reminder that someone out there still saw you, still cared.

And what kept me focused—beyond the letters—was the finish line: graduating from boot camp and starting "A School," our next phase of training. That's when we'd finally find out where we'd be stationed for the next 24 weeks. What ship we'd be assigned to. What life we'd be living.

When I got the orders, I had no clue what to expect. Meridian,

Mississippi? All I knew was the spelling: M-I-crooked letter-crooked letter-I, crooked letter-crooked letter-I, humpback-humpback-I. I'd never been that deep into the South, and the most I knew about it was slavery and Freaknik. But I didn't care. At that point, I was just proud to be a military man. I was doing something with my life.

And the best part? Bunkin got stationed with me.

He was going to A School in Meridian too, studying to become a barber. I was assigned to run the ship store—handling the vending machines, laundry for officers, the register, managing inventory— basically whatever needed to be done. We had different classes, but we were still bunkmates. That meant we were rocking together every day, all day. And I was grateful. Because no matter where I was, I wasn't alone. My brother was still with me.

It didn't take long for Mississippi to show its true colors. I saw the KKK for the first—and only—time while stationed there.

We were warned not to wear our uniforms outside the base. They said it could make us a target. But come on, in a Navy town, wearing your uniform came with perks—discounts, respect, attention from the ladies. Why wouldn't we take advantage of that? And besides, I'm from New York. Ain't nobody about to tell me how to move.

So one night, me, Bunkin, and a few of the guys hit a local bar in full uniform. We were vibing—drinking, laughing, music going, just having a good time. Then I noticed a group of white men walk in. Something was off. They weren't just looking at us—they were mean mugging, like we didn't belong. You could feel the hate in their eyes.

One of our white shipmates leaned over and quietly said, "We need to get up outta here."

We brushed it off at first. We weren't about to let a few looks ruin our night. But twenty minutes later, he said it again—this time more serious. That same group of men had left the bar, and when we walked outside, we saw them again—across the street. But now, they had on full KKK hoods. No cap.

They didn't say a word. Just stood there, watching us. We stayed cool, didn't panic, didn't make a scene—but we got the hell out of there fast. That night was a wake-up call. I might've been a proud Navy man, but out there in the deep South, in 1996, that uniform didn't mean protection. To some people, I was just another Black man they wanted to intimidate—or worse.

But I didn't fold. Not then. Not ever.

When you enlist in the Navy, your role is determined by what's needed on a specific ship. Toward the end of A School, Bunkin and I found out we were both headed to Norfolk, Virginia—but to different ships. He was assigned to the USS Stennis (CVN 74), and I was headed to the USS Dwight D. Eisenhower (CVN 69). Both of us were Ship Servicemen, or SHs, but we were finally being split up.

That shit hit hard.

We had enlisted together with plans to do those four years side by side, then reevaluate if we'd reenlist. Now I had to roll solo? In a place I didn't know, surrounded by people I didn't trust yet? I was almost ready to call it quits. But just like when I left my Moms' crib, this was the next level of manhood. I had to hold my own.

And let me tell you, manhood got tested real quick.

Petty Officer Willie Hall was part of the crew that welcomed me onboard. He was maybe a little older than me, pigeon-toed, bowlegged, heavy southern accent—you know the type. The kind of dude who would clown you all night at the cookout while holding a beer in one hand and talking shit with the other. He seemed cool... at first.

But then I heard them joking in the laundry room:

"New York City in the building!"

"Oh, we got us a tough guy now."

That's when Hall looked at me and said, "If you join our squad, you gotta ride the dryer."

I paused. What?

They opened up the industrial dryer and expected me to get in. Apparently, "riding the dryer" was some twisted welcome ritual. Nah. Not me.

The last time someone forced me into a space I didn't belong, I was five years old—tricked into a manhole, had the cover dropped on my head, and left with stitches. That wasn't happening again.

They thought it was funny—grabbing at me, laughing, trying to force me inside. But they quickly found out I wasn't the one to play with. Martial arts mode kicked in. I started swinging. I was tagging everybody. I wasn't there to be hazed, and I damn sure wasn't climbing in no damn dryer.

Eventually, Hall had to step in and calm things down. His laugh echoed through the room as he told everyone to fall back.

"We just messin' with you, shipmate. But okay—we see you about that life."

Yeah, they saw me.

That moment earned me respect. From that day on, they knew not to bring me no bullshit. I didn't back down, and that mattered in an environment like that. Hall and I even grew close. And it was through him that I met her—Nikita.

She reminded me of Chilli from TLC. Don't ask me why. They didn't look exactly alike, but something about her vibe gave me that Chilli energy. Maybe it was her soft-spoken confidence, or her slim frame and deep eyes. Whatever it was, I was drawn to her.

Hall swore up and down she wouldn't give me the time of day.

"She ain't gone want you," he'd say.

Why?

"'Cause you a slick-talking New Yorker."

But that's exactly why I knew I would win her over.

You can't tell a dude from Queens what he can't do. That just makes us go harder. I had already survived the coldest winters, the deepest pain, and boot camp—there was no way I wasn't about to shoot my shot. And sure enough, I got her attention.

We started vibing—hanging out, grabbing food, sneaking off to each other's apartments. We kept it on the low because dating onboard your ship was technically against the rules. But off-duty? We were damn near inseparable.

Still, even though we spent a lot of time together, we didn't know each other the way people in serious relationships should. We were both introverts. We could sit in the same room for hours without saying a word and be perfectly content. Our real chemistry came out around friends, music, or drinks. But deep, consistent communication? Nah... we weren't there yet.

That would eventually catch up with us.

Our connection may have had its gaps, but it didn't stop life from happening.

When Nikita told me she was pregnant, my first reaction wasn't fear—it was confusion. Me? A father? I was just getting settled in the Navy. I had just gotten my bearings in a place where I barely knew anyone. And now I was about to be responsible for someone?

Still, I embraced it. The weight of that responsibility hit differently. For once, someone was going to need me. And I swore I would never be like my father. I would be present, involved, nothing like the man who put my mother through hell. This child deserved better—and I was determined to be better.

We made plans. She'd go back to East Texas where her support system was, and I'd stay on duty in Virginia. It wasn't ideal, but at least I'd have a steady paycheck. The plan was that once I got stationed somewhere more permanent, I'd make a way to be close.

But I wasn't there for the birth.

That still stings.

I got a call that she was in labor and I was stuck on the ship. I couldn't get leave approved in time. The first time I saw my son, he was already here. And even though I wasn't there to cut the cord or hold him in the hospital, the moment I laid eyes on him, something shifted inside me.

Dante.

I didn't know it at the time, but that boy would become one of the greatest teachers I'd ever have.

Looking at him, it was like seeing a new version of me—one untouched by pain, unscarred by trauma. And that terrified me. I didn't want him to ever feel what I felt. I didn't want him to see the things I had seen, or grow up with the weight of survival on his chest.

I wanted him to laugh. To play. To know what it meant to be safe.

So, I promised myself that I would build the kind of life for him that I never had. And that meant making some tough choices— including where I'd live, who I'd become, and what kind of man I needed to be if I was going to raise one.

But the road ahead was more complicated than I imagined.

By January 1998, my time in the Navy was winding down. I had just one month left before my official discharge. Dante was nearly a year old, and my entire world was sitting at a crossroads.

Do I move to East Texas and be a full-time father—even if that meant sacrificing my personal ambitions? Or do I follow the tug on my spirit telling me there was more to life than settling?

Nikita and I weren't solid. We had a child, but the relationship? It was fragile at best. Still, the idea of leaving my son— intentionally—made me feel like I was turning into the very man I swore I wouldn't become.

There were options. I could've worked at Pilgrim's chicken plant. Or tried to get on at Exxon, where Nikita's father held a senior role. They made good money, no doubt. But I knew myself. Factory life wasn't for me. I wasn't built to clock in and out, day after day, wondering if this was all life had for me.

I had joined the military to break out of that cycle, not to fall back into it.

Toine kept calling me from Atlanta, pushing the dream: "Bro, come down here. Let's run it up." He already had a place, and Atlanta had always felt like a city full of energy and potential. Freaknik had put it on the map. Black excellence was in the air down there, from the culture to the music to the movement. It wasn't just a city—it was a vibe. And that vibe was calling my name.

But so was my son.

I wrestled with that choice day and night. One road gave me presence. The other offered me possibility. Stay and provide stability, or go and chase purpose?

In the end, I chose me. For the first time in my life, I chose me. I called Nikita and told her I was moving to Atlanta. I needed to become a man on my own terms so that I could one day come back and be the father Dante deserved.

It wasn't easy. And it damn sure wasn't perfect. But I believed— deep down—that the legacy I wanted to build had to start with a leap of faith.

And that leap began in Atlanta.

CHAPTER 7
"I'M SLIPPIN', I'M FALLIN'..."

Life has a way of bringing you full circle. I was back sleeping on a pallet on the floor—this time at my boy Toine's house. He had a two-bedroom apartment in College Park, a suburb just outside of Atlanta. Bunkin and I were crashing there until we found jobs and got back on our feet. There was nothing "suburban" about it, though. Not in the traditional sense anyway. We were in the hood, sharing the apartment with the water bugs that came to visit regularly. But we didn't care. We were young, dumb, and excited to see what Atlanta was really like outside of Freaknik.

We called Atlanta "baby New York" because so many New York niggas had moved there. Atlanta was Black. They had culture. The Olympics had just been held in the A the year before. Crazy thing is, I was actually in Atlanta during the Olympics. After I injured myself in the Navy, I was placed on limited duty. During that time, I acquired my CDL and was assigned as a bus driver for Olympic athletes. Definitely a once-in-a-lifetime opportunity. Atlanta had a special energy, and we felt it. We loved every part of it.

That wasn't particularly true for Nikita. I was so focused on finding my own peace and joy that I convinced myself I could still be a good father—even long-distance. Nikita was trying to be cordial with me, and I was doing my best to be cordial with her. But at the same time, I could hear Dante crying in the background during phone calls, and I was missing him like crazy. Add to that the inevitable expenses that come with raising a baby—and I was coming up short. That sent me into straight hustle mode. Her father was there for her, but Nikita and Dante were still my responsibility. Period! I wasn't about to let her or my son go without.

It sounded good in my head. But in reality, I wasn't taking care of them like I wanted to—or needed to. I was fighting to survive and eat, all while knowing I had a responsibility I wasn't handling the way I should've been. And then it hit me: I had spent most of my life trying to be nothing like my father, yet here I was doing the exact same thing he did. I wasn't being present—physically or financially—for my son.

Things eventually began to turn around for me in Atlanta. By 2001, Toine, Bunkin, and I had a three-bedroom apartment in Gwinnett County, a suburb about forty minutes northeast of Atlanta. I landed a job doing customer service in a call center for Nextel—the phone company that would later become Sprint. I even had a little prepaid Powertell phone. Powertell came before Nextel. Back then, if you had a prepaid phone, you thought you were doing something.

I also had a girlfriend—and she had a child. That didn't sit too well with Nikita. It wasn't that she was jealous of the girlfriend. It's that she felt like I was taking care of my girl's child while our child had needs that weren't being met. And I can see how she felt that way. I was miles away from the child I created but just minutes away from this new woman's child that, by all accounts, wasn't even my responsibility.

My responsibilities at work had grown, and I was promoted to Project Manager. This meant I'd be relocating to the company's headquarters in Reston, Virginia, about twenty-five minutes outside of Washington, D.C. It also meant I was once again stepping out on my own—leaving Toine and Bunkin. The brothers were being separated again. But it had to happen. This was a necessary step toward entering the next phase of adulthood.

The woman I was dating wanted to move with me, so we took that step together. We packed up and started the next chapter in the nation's capital.

Not long after our arrival in Virginia, the relationship ended. She decided to go back to Atlanta. Meanwhile, I was flourishing professionally. I was making better money, had stock options, and was really getting my shit together. Karate Kareem had evolved into

Corporate America Kareem—with a real nine-to-five and a title.

But then the guilt started to creep in.

I was trying to be this great long-distance dad to a growing boy I missed every single day. Moms was in my ear too:

"This ain't right, Kareem. You ain't never try with that girl the way you needed to."

And she was right. I never truly gave my relationship with Nikita the real chance it deserved. And I knew I was neglecting my son.

I wanted to be a family—the white picket fence, the dog, the so-called American Dream. And after some serious thought, prayer, and reflection on the guilt I was feeling, I realized what I had to do:

I have no choice but to give this shit a try. I need to be with my lady—the mother of my child. Most importantly, I need to be with my son.

Nikita and Dante moved to Northern Virginia less than a year after I got there.

I will never forget September 11, 2001.

At the time, Nikita, Dante, and I were living in Chantilly, Virginia, just under ten miles south of my old apartment in Reston. Like the rest of the country, I was glued to the news, trying to make sense of what I was seeing.

A plane had crashed into the North Tower of the World Trade Center?

Hijacked?

A terrorist attack??

I was in the breakroom at work, watching everything unfold live on TV while on the phone with Moms. She worked in Manhattan—three blocks from Wall Street—right near where the first plane hit. I could hear the rumbling in the background as she spoke. And then, right in front of the world's eyes, the second plane hit the South

Tower.

My concern turned into full-blown panic.

I screamed into the phone, telling her to get out of there—"Run! Go home now!"

My mother had already lived through enough for two lifetimes. I needed my superhero to be safe. But then the phones in New York City went down.

I kept calling her back to back, praying she'd pick up and tell me she was okay.

She never did.

And then came the third crash.

The Pentagon.

That one hit even closer. Chantilly, where I lived and where my son's daycare was, was only twenty minutes from the Pentagon. Nikita called me immediately and told me, "Go get our son." I didn't hesitate—I left and rushed to pick Dante up.

That was the first, but not the last time, I'd rush to get my son to safety.

Once I got home, with Nikita and Dante safe, I kept calling Moms every fifteen minutes. No answer. Nothing but a sinking pit in my stomach and hours of agonizing silence. The news kept playing on loop—death, destruction, and devastation. I didn't know if my mother was one of those people trapped in the towers. I didn't know if I'd ever hear her voice again.

I cried like a baby.

Six hours later, my phone finally rang. It was Moms. She had made it home safely after walking all the way from Manhattan across the Brooklyn Bridge to get back to Brooklyn. And if you're from New York, you know we walk everywhere—but no one walks ten miles over that bridge for fun.

I was relieved. Grateful.

But I also knew many families wouldn't be so lucky.

I had blossomed at Nextel, but soon moved on to a new opportunity at EchoStar Communications—a satellite television equipment distributor that would later become DISH Network. I was hired as a project manager, and one of my first major wins was helping lead the launch of what I believe was the first satellite dish—at least, the first to my knowledge.

With the increase in pay, I moved my family into a nice townhome. Nikita had never felt comfortable in our old Chantilly apartment anyway—my ex-girlfriend had lived there with me before heading back to Atlanta. So this move was a fresh start for all of us.

The new spot was a two-level townhouse with two bedrooms and two and a half baths. Downstairs had the living room, kitchen, and half bath, while the upstairs had the bedrooms and two full baths. I was trying. I really was. I wanted to build the life I had always dreamed of—the house, the dog, the family. And yes, we even had a dog: a chihuahua mutt named Jigga. Of course we named him after Jay-Z. I'm from New York—what more can I say?

That dog was something else. He used to bite the shit out of me and anyone else who got too close. Eventually, I had to get rid of him, but hey—I tried.

Around that same time, I made an effort to repair something else too:

My relationship with my father.

At the time, he had less than a year left on his sentence at Rikers Island for possession with intent to distribute. That was his usual charge. He was never locked up for distribution itself—because truth be told, he wasn't any good at being a drug dealer. He got high on his own supply, every single time.

But my Moms—divorced from him and all—still loved that man. And she, along with Nikita, convinced me to at least go visit him. Maybe, just maybe, there was still a chance to salvage something before it was too late.

Let me be real with you—Rikers Island is not a place you just go visit. I wouldn't wish that trip on anyone unless it was absolutely necessary.

Visiting someone in prison is hard enough. But visiting a man you have so much anger, pain, and trauma attached to? That's another beast. And it's not like the prison system makes it any easier. They treat you like you're the criminal.

Pat-downs. Bag checks. Disrespectful guards.

Even for New Yorkers, they were rude as hell.

But I went.

For the man who stole my clarinet money and left me stranded outside the music store.

For the man who put hands on my Moms.

For the man who made me have to defend her when I was just a child.

Yep. I was going through all of that—for him.

I needed to know where his head was at. I needed to know if he was finally ready to be a man. Because I was a man now. I had a woman, a child, a career. I had a new life—and he wasn't coming anywhere near it unless I knew he was right.

As always, Pops tried to charm his way through. He had jokes, that slick talk. And he came out dressed for the part: kufi on his head, full-on "last Muslim" energy. He was deep into the Qur'an now. That was his thing when he was locked up—no pork, religious devotion, fasting, all of it.

And what do you know—he and Moms were all laughs and smiles.

Still carrying on like he hadn't done a thing wrong. She really did love that man.

But I was focused. I didn't come to play. I told him directly:

"If you want to see your grandson, you gotta show me that you've changed."

Surprisingly, by the end of the visit, I felt open enough to extend the olive branch. I said, "When you get out, reach out to me. I'll make sure you get to meet your grandson." I wasn't making promises, but I was willing to move forward. It felt like a step in the right direction.

About a week after his release, my father actually did call me.

He was staying with one of my aunts in Brooklyn and had reached out through Moms to get my number. We spoke for maybe 30 or 40 minutes, and he sounded good. Still slick-talking, still confident—but saying all the right things:

"I'm ready to see you. I wanna see my grandson. I'm gonna get my life together."

I asked when he wanted to come, and we picked a date. I sent him money via Western Union—enough for either an Amtrak or Greyhound ticket, plus some food and pocket cash. If the ticket was $150, I probably sent him $250. No strings attached—just a genuine offer to come see his family.

And then...

That was the last time I ever heard from him.

The day he was supposed to arrive came and went. No call. No show. No explanation.

Moms hadn't heard from him. My aunts didn't know where he was.

But I knew. Deep down, I already knew.

He was back in the streets.

No clarification. No closure.

Just another chapter in a long story of broken promises.

But this time—he didn't just leave me outside the music store.

He left me standing there as a grown man, with a girlfriend, a son, and a heart wide open...

Only to walk out of my life again.

After maybe a year, Nikita was growing more and more homesick. On top of that, our chemistry wasn't what it needed to be. I was trying to do whatever I could to please her and be with our son. I didn't want to be without Dante anymore, so her moving back to East Texas while I stayed on the East Coast just wasn't an option.

After long conversations and some arguments, I finally said, fuck it.

"You wanna move to Texas?"

I wasn't moving to East Texas—and Nikita knew that. But my job had an opening for a remote position in Dallas, and I was able to transfer. I was basically working from home, before working from home was even a thing. It was only two and a half hours from Nikita's family, and Dallas was big enough for me to establish myself and try and take over.

My first time there, Nikita's uncles made a hell of a first impression, so that made me a little more comfortable about relocating to the "Triple D." But that meant the move I was making was causing me to leave my family. Virginia was good for me because I was only four or five hours from New York and eight or nine hours from Atlanta. I was in between my Moms up north and my brothers down south. Leaving them was the ultimate sacrifice, but I did it for my new family. I did it so that I could continue waking up and seeing my son.

Dante was the reason I moved to Texas.

For four weeks, we lived in a nice apartment in North Dallas, off Parker Rd and the Dallas North Tollway. A clean two-bedroom spot overlooking the pool. Growing up in Rochdale, my apartment faced other apartments. And we damn sure didn't have no pool. No projects in New York had pools. Growing up, we only had city pools. I remember going to Flushing Meadow Park and Astoria under the bridge—Moms took me there as often as she could in the summers.

But now? I could afford to live in a nice area, in a nice crib, with a nice view. I made that happen. And that's not something my father could've said.

My mindset was simple: as long as I'm nothing like him, I'm doing okay.

Renting a house was one thing. But owning a home? That was a different conversation—a conversation I wasn't trying to have. I didn't think we were ready for that kind of commitment. But Nikita did. My hesitation wasn't just financial—it was emotional too. We weren't vibing like we should. But when we did the math, owning a home actually made more sense than renting. We were paying $2,500 a month for rent, but once I got approved, the mortgage would be just $1,200.

Choice Homes had a first-time homebuyer program, and I was approved for a house in DeSoto, Texas, a suburb about fifteen minutes south of Dallas. On May 9, 2003, Kareem Thomson—the kid from Southside Jamaica Queens, Rochdale Village, Section 1 Building 2—became a homeowner in DeSoto, Texas.

The same kid who used to hang out in Ms. Knors' office for fudge and butter cookies. Who slept on pallets so much it felt normal. Who hustled outside of Key Foods hoping to eat and help Moms with car fare. Who was homeless. Who got bit by bedbugs in a motel.

I owned a home.

Not an apartment lease. Not a sublet. A house.

Was the situation ideal? No.

Were we ready? Honestly, I didn't think so.

But God allowed it anyway—and I was proud.

I felt like I had outdone my father. My choices didn't leave us homeless or put us out on the street. My credit and income didn't disqualify me—they qualified me to move my family from an apartment to a house with a yard. With neighbors, not neighbors above or below us.

And whether or not I was happy in my relationship, I was holding it down. I was making sure my family had a roof over their heads. He didn't do that.

And finally—like I'd promised myself—I was nothing like my father.

My son's childhood was also nothing like that of his father's—another goal I swore I'd accomplish. Texas is different from New York, period. But that's what made me grow to love it. Dallas was slower-paced and peaceful. I dropped Dante off at school; he wasn't walking or catching the train like I did. On days he rode the bus, it was a yellow school bus—not the MTA. His teachers knew he had two actively present parents at home. He'd never have to beg for a loaner instrument just to live out a dream. He excelled in school. His teachers loved him. Dante never had to hang out in a teacher's office just to get cookies because he didn't have lunch money.

We had a basketball goal in the driveway, and we'd hoop right outside the house. When I was growing up in Rochdale, I had to walk blocks just to find a court. Now my son could walk out the front door and play ball with his dad.

Like me, Dante loved basketball so much that he played in a league. He wore the same jersey number as I did—#15—and played point guard like me and two-guard like Bunkin. But unlike me, Dante never had to play hungry. He had the foundation. The structure. The support I never did. Hell, maybe he'd even go on to fall in love with a cheerleader in high school too.

Purchasing the house felt like my final leap of faith in trying to make this relationship work. But I'd be lying if I said that mortgage brought us closer. It didn't. Our disagreements weren't violent or even abusive—but we weren't clicking. It wasn't always yelling or slamming doors, but it was emotional silence. The kind where two people share space but aren't really connected. We were trying, but we just weren't talking—not the way people should if they want to build a life together.

We hadn't laid the foundation. We didn't have the language. And when you don't know how to speak to one another, your emotions turn into arguments because you have nothing else to stand on. The tension would build, and instead of looking for the root, I'd just ask, "Why are you so angry?"—never realizing I was part of the answer. Add the stress of being young parents figuring it out as we went, and we were both drowning, silently.

Still, I was trying. Trying to do what my father never did—stay. Be a father. Hold it down.

But I was also leaning harder into the things that brought me joy.

While EchoStar paid the bills, I was getting more into lifestyle marketing. Promoting parties was something I'd started dabbling in back in Atlanta, and Dallas was full of opportunities. While promoting in the ATL, I met Nick Storm—a lifestyle specialist and marketing guru with Hpnotiq, the blue liqueur that had the early 2000s in a chokehold. We stayed in touch. And when I realized Hpnotiq didn't have anyone representing them in Texas, I saw my lane.

I called Nick. Next thing you know, I'm Hpnotiq's Dallas brand ambassador. My job? Make people drink. Be in the clubs. Pop bottles. Get the product in people's hands and faces. And I was getting paid to do it.

By 2004, about a year after we touched down in Dallas, "Mr. Hpnotik" was born.

Corporate Kareem paid the bills. But Mr. Hpnotik fed my soul.

The clubs. The culture. The nightlife. The entertainment bag. That's what fueled me. I was outside. I was making a name. I was chasing something that felt more me than any 9-5 ever could. But while I was chasing that bag, my relationship was falling apart.

Promoting meant I came home at 2 or 3 in the morning. That meant Nikita was home, alone, with our son. And while I thought I was doing what I had to do to keep us afloat, I wasn't really present.

Then things got real.

EchoStar ended my remote position. I was given two options: move back to North Virginia and continue in-person, or leave the company. As much as I wanted to be close to Moms and my people up north, I wasn't about to walk out my son's life again. I couldn't leave Dallas.

So I let EchoStar go—and leaned fully into the hustle.

Hpnotiq paid anywhere between $200 to $400 a night. I knew the mortgage was three $400 gigs. That's not including utilities, food, or diapers. But I was outside every night, submitting expense reports and making it work.

And that's when I started moving reckless.

I was partying. Drinking. Popping bottles. And, for a brief moment—popping ecstasy pills. I'd drive from downtown to DeSoto drunk and high, just praying I made it home. I thank God I did. Every single time.

One night, I wasn't so lucky.

I was driving Nikita's brand-new red Mustang when a drunk driver hit me. The car flipped. I blacked out, came to just long enough to see the guy running from the scene. I couldn't move. All I could do was crawl out and pray.

When Nikita and Dante arrived, they were scared out of their minds. I could've died. Their father, their partner—gone. That shook me. I knew God spared me that night.

And then, just like that, Hpnotiq cut the budget.

At the same time, things between me and Nikita reached a boiling point. It was toxic—not abusive, not physical—but not healthy. And I wasn't going to wait for it to escalate. I wasn't going to let my son grow up watching his parents fight.

He wasn't going to do what I did—protect his mother from me.

I had to be real.

"This isn't going to work."

I thought moving across the country was the ultimate sacrifice. But letting go of my family—watching them move back to East Texas—was the hardest decision I've ever made.

My ego told me I could make it work. That a two-and-a-half-hour drive was nothing. That I could still be present, still be involved, still be better than my father. But the truth? I couldn't even afford to take care of my family. I couldn't even keep us together.

Dante was now living with his mom. And I was, again, on the outside looking in. That feeling of failure? It hit me hard.

I failed my son. I failed Nikita. I failed my Moms. I failed myself.

How am I better than my father if I can't even be in my son's life every day?

We never poured into that house. We didn't even buy curtains. And when she left and took the furniture, the emptiness in the house reflected the emptiness in me. I didn't buy anything new. I didn't make it a home. It became a bachelor pad—a shell I came home to after long nights out, trying to outrun the guilt.

But what hurt the most wasn't the silence in the house.

It was the silence of not hearing my son's laughter.

I knew I had to go harder. I wasn't leaving Dallas. I wasn't leaving Dante. No way this New York nigga was about to give up just because life got hard.

My life had always been hard.

Even with no Hpnotiq budget, I was still in the clubs popping bottles, spending my last dollar just to maintain the image of "Mr.

Hpnotik." In April 2005, for my 30th birthday, I threw a huge celebrity bash. DJ Envy came through. Gloria Velez was there. The party was packed. But I let most people in free.

My ego cost me everything.

After a few more failed promotions, the truth became undeniable: I was broke. My brother Bunkin had moved to Dallas in June 2005, and he was doing what he could to help. But by December, I lost the house.

My first home went into foreclosure.

I hadn't smoked up the mortgage. I just never had enough to begin with.

It felt like I was back at the bottom. Like DMX said:

"I'm slippin', I'm fallin', I can't get up."

And just like that—I was homeless again.

I had to pack all my shit into my Ford Expedition. No apartment. No plan. I was back to being that same kid from Queens who couldn't afford a place to sleep.

At least Bunkin had a place to go. He moved to Alaska with Toine, who had joined the Air Force and was stationed in Anchorage. I felt bad leaving his stuff behind when they foreclosed on the house, but there was nowhere else to put it. And Bunkin, being the real one he is, understood. Bigger battles were being fought.

Now it was just me. My truck. My thoughts. And no clear path forward.

I drove all day just to avoid stopping. But eventually, night came. I pulled into a park, parked the truck, and sat still in the silence. No gas to keep the engine running. It was cold. Too cold.

I had fucked up. Bad.

I wasn't in a motel. I wasn't at a friend's. I wasn't even on a pallet.

I was in my car.

Homeless.

Thirty years old.

And starting over.

CHAPTER 8
"ALLOW ME TO RE-INTRODUCE MYSELF..."

Vanessa was flying down I-30, weaving in and out of traffic, doing everything she could to get us to East Texas faster. We had about an hour to go, but I knew it wouldn't take that long with her behind the wheel. She wasn't playing. But for me, time stood still. Every mile felt like a lifetime. My eyes were glued to the phone, just praying Nikita would call and tell me my son was okay. I was staring at that screen like it was 9/11 all over again, waiting for Moms to call and tell me she made it out safe. But this time, the call never came. And my patience was running out.

Vanessa tried to calm me down, but I couldn't sit still. I needed to see my son.

Meanwhile, my mother's only son was essentially homeless. I didn't have a home of my own. I stayed in the house in DeSoto until the lights got cut off. Once the water stopped running and the final notices started piling up, I finally left. But until then, I was still there—stretching every ounce of time I had left. After that, I bounced between my truck and Motel 6. Eventually, I asked my girlfriend if I could move in with her.

A little over a year after Nikita and Dante moved back to East Texas, I started dating someone new. She was going to school at the University of North Texas in Denton and lived on campus. We met at Vain Lounge, where I was doing marketing and she worked as one of the "Vain Lounge Girls." Basically, a bottle girl before bottle girls were a thing. Vain was probably the first spot in Dallas to bring in eye candy for the sections.

From the start, I kept it real with her. She knew about the foreclosure. She knew I didn't have much. But she saw the hustle. She saw me moving, making a name for myself with the Mr. Hpnotik events. She believed in my potential.

We were just friends at first, but it quickly turned into something more. Still, it was humbling—hell, embarrassing—to ask my girl if I could move into her two-bedroom on-campus apartment. She had a roommate and everything. But it beat sleeping in the truck. It beat the Motel 6. So I swallowed my pride and took the help.

By 2006, I was 31 years old, living with my college girlfriend on a campus apartment, and throwing parties to survive. But I was back on the grind.

My signature parties were starting to set me apart. I got creative with the marketing — everything had to stand out. One year, my birthday flyer was designed like a credit card. Another year, it was a custom mixtape cover. I was also one of the first promoters in Dallas to bring DJ Envy to town. Even though the Hpnotiq budget had dried up, I kept using the name to build my lifestyle brand. Mr. Hpnotik was still in motion.

The promoter game gave me some wins... and plenty of losses. I found ways to land sponsors for events — some got paid back, some didn't. But I was hustling. I even threw a party in Los Angeles during NBA All-Star Weekend in 2004. That one was a big deal. Celebs like Lil' Kim, Tank, and radio legend Greg Street all pulled up. I was making noise, coast to coast.

Locally, I had a steady gig at Vain Lounge. "Steady" in the sense that I had a regular position — but the pay? That came when it came. The owners were cool though. Hustlers. They gave me creative freedom and always treated me like family. I was earning about $500 a week — two grand a month. Not much, but enough to survive.

Then came one of the biggest L's I ever took as a promoter — the night that made me walk away from that side of the game altogether.

My guy Big Chad, aka BC, and I partnered on a major event at Vain. BC ran Southern Fried Marketing — one of the most respected street promo companies in the South — so we had a solid team and a buzz. The plan was to throw a star-studded industry party with Bobby Valentino headlining. At the time, Bobby V was hot — songs like "Slow Down" and "Tell Me" had the ladies in a chokehold. "I'll meet you in the VIP" was the perfect soundtrack for what I was creating. We had everything: radio commercials (which cost real money), catered food, an ice sculpture, VIP upstairs. I wanted to bring that classic New York upscale club vibe to the Triple D.

And we thought we'd make our money back — plus some.

Except… we didn't.

People showed up, but nowhere near enough. We didn't break even, not even close. I remember sitting outside the club with BC, both of us grown-ass men, on the verge of tears. We had poured everything into that party — time, energy, reputation, money — and it flopped. For BC, it was a hit to his name. For me? It was how I ate.

That night made one thing clear: I had to pivot. My promoter days were done.

After that, I transitioned strictly into doing marketing for Vain Lounge. Then the club shut down. But one of the people connected to Vain was opening a new spot — and brought me along for the ride. I was asked to do marketing for the new club based on my track record, and my girl came with me too. She was now working at the new spot as well.

That new club? Club X. Formerly Club Life. And Club X is where everything shifted.

My usual "uniform" was a button-down shirt, jeans, and either Uptowns or Timbs. I was still that guy — shorts and Timbs in the middle of a Texas summer. Real New Yorker. But Club X was buzzing, and as the marketing guy, I like to think I played a part in that.

Then a well-known Dallas radio personality named Veda Loca walked in — and flipped my whole path on its head.

Club X had a live broadcast on Saturday nights. Veda was doing afternoons at 97.9 The Beat, and we brought her in to host the live broadcast from the club to the radio. One night, either during a break or after she wrapped, Veda ducked off for a bit and left the mic unattended. But the club was still lit — the crowd was vibing, the music was up, and we needed someone on the mic to make announcements. You know, the usual: drink specials, bartender shoutouts, hyping the crowd up.

The owner turned to me and said, "Yo, grab the mic."

I ain't hesitate. I wasn't shy, and I knew how to work a room. So I hopped on and did what needed to be done.

Veda came back and saw me on the mic.

"You tryin' to do my job now?" she joked, half laughing, half surprised.

"Nah," I said. "Just filling in."

But she wasn't done.

"Take this mic. You got a voice. Use it."

That night, I hosted the rest of the event — and I hosted my way right into a whole new job.

From that moment on, the owner realized he had a two-for-one: a marketing guy and a host. Just like that, Mr. Hpnotik the club host was born.

I believe in God's timing because I've lived it. Some of the biggest shifts in my life weren't luck or coincidence — they were divine. One of the clearest examples? I caught a flat tire. That's it. Just a flat tire.

I pulled into Walmart to buy a new tire, annoyed but handling it. While I waited, I met a brother named Preston Rich. He was sharp — suit, confident posture, carried himself like a boss. We got to talking, just casual. Southern hospitality. Then it turned deeper. Turned spiritual.

Preston asked what I did, and I told him about my marketing and hosting. But the real connection came when I found out he was an Air Force vet and I told him I served in the Navy. Not only that, he was from Virginia — where I had been stationed. Small world, right?

Turned out, Preston was a project manager at PepsiCo. He led a team of IT consultants and mentioned they might have an opening. That was the moment. I told him about my project management background and how I was looking for something more stable to get back on my feet. He told me to send him my résumé.

I went home, sent it over immediately — and landed the interview.

The interview went great. I was confident, professional, and ready to work. And I got the job.

Now picture this: Mr. Hpnotik — the club host who had been living on campus with his girlfriend just months ago — was now leading multi-million-dollar initiatives at PepsiCo headquarters in Plano, Texas. I was making $130,000 a year as a project manager.

All because I caught a flat tire.

That was nothing but GOD.

Even though I was back in corporate America — pulling in nearly $5,000 every two weeks — my heart still beat for entertainment. I wasn't ready to let go of Mr. Hpnotik. So, I did both. Monday through Friday, I was Corporate Kareem. Nights and weekends, I was The People's Host.

My guy Dray Williams — who would later help run my foundation — had formed the Major League DJs, a powerhouse squad made up of some of the hottest in the city: DJ Klassik, DJ Ski, DJ Chubb, DJ Passion. And of course, yours truly on the mic. If it wasn't us or OGs like DJ Steve Nice, DJ TDK, or DJ Phil on the flyer, nobody was showing up. Respectfully.

I was back in hustle mode. Climbing out of debt. Recovering from that foreclosure. Hosting major celebrity events. Still popping Hpnotiq bottles like they were cutting me a check. And I'll admit it — I had a bad habit of living beyond my means. Not something I'm proud of, but back then, the image mattered more than the reality. I thought the public perception of success was just as important as actual success.

Eventually, I got my own place. In 2007, I moved into a dope crib in Addison, right off Montfort Drive. It was perfect — close to PepsiCo, far enough from the noise, and finally my own again. It wasn't just about having a roof; it was about reclaiming stability. I didn't have to wait for someone to buzz me through a gate or navigate around a roommate anymore. I was 32, grown, grinding, and rebuilding. One brick at a time.

I was doing better — but I still wanted more.

K104 — the #1 hip hop and R&B station in Dallas — was holding a city-wide contest for their next on-air personality to join the "Skip Cheatham and the Playground Morning Show." This was the shot of a lifetime. I just didn't think it was my shot. I was still knee-deep in club hosting. I didn't see myself as a radio guy. But the streets did. Everybody kept telling me to go for it.

Skip Cheatham was the man. Program Director. Host. Bentley-driving. Big-time energy. When he pulled up, he moved the city. The idea of working beside him was wild — and $50,000 a year for a starting radio gig? That was cool. But compared to what I was making at PepsiCo, it was pennies. Still, people were in my ear heavy. Even DC Cole, who helped run Flava TV with Skip and was tight with me, was pushing me to go all in. So I did what I always do: I got creative.

I flipped the whole thing into a campaign. My submission video was like a presidential election promo. The intro had Jay-Z's "PSA" sample: "Allow me to reintroduce myself..." and I came in full throttle — "My name is HPNOTIK!" I dressed the part, stood in a studio, added clips of me hosting packed events, and showed why the job wasn't just for me — it was already mine. I even remixed Boosie's "Wipe Me Down," calling out every name on the morning show. It was catchy, authentic, and 100% me.

When I prayed on it, God said, "Go for it." I didn't care if the job paid less — purpose was calling.

It came down to me and KC Mac, a comedian with serious chops. We both had to audition live on air. I was nervous as hell. I walked into K104 at 6 a.m.rocking my signature NYC fit — button-down, jeans, Timbs — and hoped I wouldn't bomb. KC killed his. Dude was hilarious. Me? I had the streets and a unique campaign, but my polish wasn't there yet. Still, I gave it my all.

Then, Skip made the announcement live on air: "I'm doing something different. I'm giving BOTH of them a contract!"

I was stunned.

The kid from Southside Jamaica Queens... was about to be on the biggest morning show in Dallas? The People's Host — who wasn't even trying to get into radio — had just hosted his way into K104?

But here's the twist: the job didn't start at $50,000. It started at $10 an hour.

See, I wasn't ready. I didn't have the radio polish yet. So Skip put me on overnights to learn the board, the breaks, and the format. When that proved rocky, I got reassigned to the K104 Street Team. That's where I learned how to really speak to the city.

Guys like C Hawk and J Rudd showed me the ropes — how to hit a clean break, how to control the mic, how to show up in every neighborhood from Oak Cliff to Fort Worth with presence and energy. We passed out movie tickets, free gas, and swag, but more than that, we connected. K104 was the streets, and the streets were me.

Once I got my rhythm, I was put back on the air.

I had officially reintroduced myself.

CHAPTER 9
"WELL MARRY ME THEN…"

Despite the money not being great, life was okay. Bunkin had made his way back to Texas while I was hosting clubs. He fell in love with Texas after coming to one of my signature parties. We had a two-bedroom apartment in Irving, a suburb west of Dallas, not far from Grand Prairie where K104 was located at the time.

My relationship, however, was not going well. I was feeling myself, but we weren't exactly feeling each other. We were both checked out—barely speaking, barely connecting. But then it went really left.

It's February 2007. My girlfriend told me she wanted to go on a girls' trip—or maybe it was back to her hometown or something like that. Like I said, I was already emotionally detached. I didn't check in much while she was gone, but I remember calling and getting no answer. I suspected something was off. I had been caught stepping out before, so I wasn't about to do too much digging. But still… something wasn't right.

Then one of my boys from New York called me. He was in Las Vegas for NBA All-Star Weekend.

"Yo, I just saw your girl."

I was like, "Nah, she's on a girls' trip."

"I'm telling you, bro. I'm looking at her right now. She's in a store—with some dude."

She never once mentioned Vegas. I didn't want to believe it, but then he sent me a picture.

It was her.

Not only did she lie about where she was going, but she was with another dude—and this dude just happened to work for the competition. Yeah. The rival morning show at K104's biggest competitor. I was so loyal to the brand that it felt like betrayal on top of betrayal.

I called and texted her with no response. So I sent one final message: "I know you're in the store with a dude. You got me confused—I can get both of y'all touched."

Out of line. Out of character. That was my ego and hurt talking.

Still no response.

So, I said, okay, bet. Let me show her how far my reach goes.

I had my guys approach her—with me on the phone. They walked up and said, "You need to get on this phone." She did. And I went off. I blacked out.

"I could have both y'all duct-taped right now. I don't know who you think you're messing with!"

It was bad. Thank God for Bunkin. He talked me down off that ledge. That situation could've gone a completely different way— career-ending, or worse.

She came back home that Sunday or Monday. We talked. And obviously, we broke up.

But it didn't end there.

The guy she cheated with? He was on the radio. Their morning show wasted no time airing it out. By that Tuesday or Wednesday, their entire show was about how he "stole somebody's girl" in Vegas.

My phone was blowing up.

It was live radio. Morning drive-time. If you were headed to work, dropping off kids, or just listening between 6 and 10am—and you knew me—you didn't need to hear a name to know who they were talking about.

I was livid.

For one, I'm Mr. Hpnotik. Don't play with my name. Two, I'm from New York. Don't play with me, period. And three, I was all in for K104. This was like the Bloods and Crips. Radio competition in Dallas was that real.

So I did what my ego told me to do—I hopped in the whip and headed straight to Valley View Mall where their station used to be. I was about to walk into that studio and confront whoever was behind that mic.

That could've been the end of my life—or at the very least, my career. Again, BC stepped in and talked me down. I'm grateful for that. Eventually, I had to sit down with both parties and apologize for my immaturity.

K104 is where I transitioned from Mr. Hpnotik to DJ Kayotik. I'll get to that in a second.

At the time, I was on-air teasing my DJ debut. Up to that point, I had only been heard—not seen—in the streets. So I'd go on the mic and tell the city, "Get ready, it's coming. You've heard me tear the clubs down with my voice, now you're about to see me tear the tables down."

The streets were ready. The anticipation was building.

And I did terribly.

I'll never forget my debut as DJ Kayotik. Early 2008, Opus Lounge, with K104's night host Catdaddy emceeing. I wasn't trash as a DJ, but I was definitely nervous—and clearly unprepared. I played the full version of almost every song. One remix I dropped had a Gucci Mane verse on it.

Catdaddy leaned over and said, "Damn, I didn't even know

Gucci Mane was on this record."

That was a wake-up call. I had been relying solely on my voice. But now, I had to figure out how to use my voice and play music—at the same time.

I left Opus Lounge feeling like shit.

But I wasn't about to let that stop me.

Tell me I'm bad at something, and I'll become one of the best at it. That's how I'm wired. So, I studied the craft. I reached out to DJs I respected—pioneers like DJ Phil, DJ Steve Nice, DJ Kid Capri, DJ TDK. I asked them to school me on the principles of being a real DJ.

And I wasn't looking for shortcuts or cheat codes. I didn't want to be a push-button DJ.

The technology was evolving—controllers, Serato, all that—but I wanted to learn the right way. From the ground up. So I bought two Technics 1200s and a Rane mixer. No shade to DJs who use digital equipment, but if I was going to rock a party next to legends like Steve Nice or Biz Markie (rest in peace), I needed to know they respected me the same way I respected them.

Those two letters in front of my name? "DJ"? I wanted them to mean something.

After putting in the work and sharpening my skill set, I earned it. DJ Kayotik wasn't just a name—I was out here earning my spot. I was killing clubs. My name was hot in the streets. If a party was popping in Dallas, chances are I was spinning it.

But while my career as a DJ was taking off, my station checks weren't adding up. I was still making $10 an hour at K104, and that wasn't cutting it—especially considering I was living outside my means. I had an apartment downtown at the Mosaic. Rooftop pool and everything.

As nice as the apartment was, nothing was nicer than the phone call I got one day while I was working.

I was at Tephejez Jazz Bar, downtown Dallas, hosting a music industry event. My phone rang. It was Bunkin.

"You won't believe who I found."

"Who?"

"Vanessa Rose."

I stepped outside the club. I was all ears.

"She friended me on Facebook," Bunkin said. "Here's your chance!"

He was joking, saying he had to make sure she wasn't fat now. But I didn't care what she looked like. I just wanted to talk to her.

I had never stopped looking for Vanessa. And I mean really looking. I even paid for one of those people-finder sites. Came up with nothing. So when Bunkin said she was back on the grid? I was on it.

After they exchanged a few words, he sent me her page. I sent the friend request immediately—followed by a message. She responded right away. As soon as I saw that notification, I called her.

Forget the event I was hosting. That could wait.

I was talking a mile a minute. I let it be known: I had been looking for her. And the timing couldn't have been more perfect. She was single but dating. And I was all the way single.

Truth is, even if I hadn't been single, whoever I was with would've been out the picture instantly. No offense to them—but they weren't Vanessa Rose. She was the one.

We started talking every day. Texting. Calling. Catching up. That went on for months. Eventually, I told her I was coming home for a family reunion—and I wanted her to come with me.

Just like the first time I met her parents.

I was a little nervous about what she looked like. Not because I didn't think she was beautiful—just because this was 2009, and there was no FaceTime yet. All we had were the pictures on Facebook.

I flew into LaGuardia. She was supposed to pick me up. I was standing at the terminal, and then she popped out from behind one of those little columns at the arrivals area.

And there she was.

That beautiful-ass smile. Those perfect lips. That face I never forgot. It was really her. Vanessa Rose. Sixteen years later.

Needless to say, we had an amazing time. I visited her crib in Rochdale—crazy how she ended up living there, right? Met her son. Kicked it like no time had passed.

But when it came time to leave... I couldn't do it.

I wasn't about to lose Vanessa again.

We were sitting there, drinking Jamaican rum, eating chicken—real New York vibes. And I looked her in her eyes and said:

"I would marry you tomorrow."

She laughed it off, thought I was joking.

But I wasn't. "I'm dead serious," I told her.

She smiled and said, "Well marry me then."

She didn't have to tell me twice.

Right then and there, I hopped online and pulled up the info for the Dallas Justice of the Peace. Filled out the paperwork on the spot. We applied for a marriage license while I was still in New York, sitting in her crib. When I flew back to Dallas from the reunion, Vanessa came with me.

It was a seamless transition. She had just lost her job, so the timing worked out. I promised I'd take care of her—and I meant that.

After the required three-day waiting period, we eloped. After years of praying, hoping, and searching, on March 9, 2009, Vanessa Rose officially became my wife.

I know what you're thinking—and no, the date had nothing to do with Biggie. That just happened to be the first day we were legally allowed to get married. I would've married her the moment she said "marry me then" if I could have.

She moved in and got a taste of my fancy "rib tip" dinner—out of a box, with some instant rice and a side. She thought I could cook. I wasn't about to ruin the illusion.

The only people who knew about the wedding were DC Cole and her then-husband Mario (rest in peace). They were our witnesses. DC even bought us our first wedding rings since it all happened so fast. Not even Bunkin knew.

And he was rightfully pissed.

I get it. Without him, I wouldn't have found her again. He had every right to feel a way. It caused some tension between us, but we worked through it.

I didn't even tell Nikita or Dante. And we got married the day after Dante's birthday.

I'm sure I spoke to him and sent something. But in hindsight, that's something I regret. That kind of milestone? I should've handled that with more care. Those are the lessons I'd eventually apply with my daughters.

Our families were happy for us, but they were also upset we didn't have a real wedding—with the bells and whistles. So, a year later, on May 10, 2010, we had a full wedding ceremony. The tux. The cake. The celebration.

My brother Bunkin was my best man, like he always had been in life. I wanted Dante to stand next to me too, but after the way I mishandled communicating my elopement to him and Nikita, it just didn't work out. That still sits with me. But it also taught me to slow down, to consider how my actions affected others—especially my kids.

Shortly after we got married, Vanessa found out just how deep in the hole I was.

I hadn't filed taxes in seven years.

My credit score was in the low 500s.

I was tens of thousands of dollars in debt.

So now she's looking at me like, "Who the hell did I marry?" I'm sure there were moments she wondered if she made a mistake. I'm the same dude who talked big, hosted clubs, and drove the image of success. But underneath all that? I was barely holding on.

But my wife? She didn't fold. She rolled up her sleeves.

Vanessa helped me fix my credit. She helped me file my back taxes and get on a payment plan. She stood beside me the same way she had when we were just kids back in high school. Just like she once brought me that egg and cheese bagel when I couldn't afford lunch—Vanessa loved me enough to help me get back on my feet, again.

She's always seen the best version of me—even when I couldn't.

And this time, I promised myself: I'm not walking out of her life again.

CHAPTER 10
"AIN'T NO GOIN' HOME…"

Even with Vanessa Rose in my life for good, professionally I still had a lot left to accomplish. I had filled in for every shift on the radio. I had a weekend show. In my mind, it's time for me to become the next Greg Street and actually be able to afford this apartment. I wanted my own weekday show.

Greg Street wasn't just a radio personality—he was the blueprint. He had done the afternoon drive at K104 before moving on to Atlanta and becoming a force at V-103. He was known across the South, and his impact stretched beyond music. When I saw him pull up in a Bentley and still be that down-to-earth, community-driven brother, it gave me hope. He showed me that radio personalities could be stars, not just voices. That's the kind of success I was aiming for.

But where would they put me? Cat Daddy was already cemented at night and killing it. That man had a following. His energy was crazy, his voice was familiar, and his connection with the streets was undeniable. I wasn't trying to take his spot—I respected his lane—but I wanted my own. I knew I had something different to bring to the table. The morning show was sewed up. So, I proposed co-hosting with the new afternoon personality, who had arrived in 2008. But my Assistant Program Director, White Gary – a white man named Gary – didn't see it that way. I pitched a couple of things to him, just trying to be a full-time jock on my show or someone else's show. Gary and I had a heart-to-heart conversation about it.

My APD looked me dead in my face and said, "I know you're buzzing out here. You're an okay personality. But let's be honest: you'll never be as big as the afternoon jock. He has an 'it' factor. No shade, you're great at what you do, but you do not have 'it'."

Excuse me? You're telling me I can't be great? After GOD already said I was going to be? Like Jay-Z said, "we don't believe you, you need more people."

It wasn't a matter of whether or not there was room for growth. They weren't going to allow me to grow, because they didn't believe I was good enough to be anything more than what I was: a part-time personality making $10 an hour. If you don't believe in me, I'll show you better than I can tell you. So, I prayed on it and decided to walk away from K104. It was an amicable separation. Skip and the owner Hymen knew I was unhappy and wanted to grow. They offered me a severance package and I couldn't file unemployment.

Even with my high ass rent and my high car note, I believe in the Most High God. I knew He gave me the vision to be a radio personality, when He told me to chase the dream back when I initially applied for Skip Cheatham and the Playground. So, whether it was going to be a radio station in Longview or Tyler, Texas, I wasn't sure. What I did know for certain was that I wasn't leaving my son. It would either be a station in the vicinity, or I was gone be the hottest person in the streets until the next radio station reached out to me.

The grind was nonstop now. I'm hungrier than ever. Not just to prove them wrong, but because being a host and a DJ was my only source of income. I was in the clubs going crazy. Beamers was the hottest club in the city at this time and I was the resident DJ. On Fridays and Saturdays, and sometimes Sundays, there would be 5,000 people in the club, rocking to DJ Kayotik. You couldn't tell me shit!

Big Bink, the afternoon jock at K104's competition, 97.9 The Beat, was at Beamers every week as well. Bink was hosting the happy hour, and his guy TDK was also spinning there. I was in his ear every week, asking what was up with his station? What's the play? How can I get in? Then I learned about the non-compete clause. Once you leave a radio station, you can't work at any competing station where your former station can be heard, for a set amount of time. But I wanted him to know, when my non-compete was up, I'd be ready. Don't forget about me. I wanted him to see how I could control the club, control the culture. I'm not with K104 anymore, but don't get it twisted—I'm still him.

I stayed consistent. Kept the energy up. And finally, all that networking and patience was about to pay off.

I got the call I'd been waiting on.

It was early in the morning, and I had just gotten in from rocking Beamers around 3 a.m. My body was dead tired. Then my phone rang. It was 6:30 a.m., and I didn't recognize the number at first. I let it go to voicemail. But curiosity got the best of me, so I checked it.

"Kayotik, it's John Candy. You still wanna be on the radio?"

Wait—what?

"Absolutely," I said, immediately calling him back.

"Can you be here by 8?"

"Yes."

"Okay. See you at 8."

I rolled over and was about to go right back to sleep. That's how dead I was. But Vanessa wasn't having it.

"You ain't getting up?" she asked. "Didn't you just get a call?"

She was right. I looked at my phone again, wiped my eyes, and realized I wasn't dreaming—this was real. The PD at 97.9 The Beat had just called me for an on-air audition. I jumped out the bed and boogied straight to the mall, threw on something decent, and headed up there.

John Candy came out like, "You ready? I'm throwing you in live on the air."

Wait, what??

I hadn't been on-air in over a year. I was rusty as hell. But I knew this was the moment. So, I took a breath, put on the headphones, and cracked the mic.

First thing I said was: "K104 IS HIP HOP..."

Oh shit. Wrong station.

John Candy came running into the studio like, "Hold up now!" I quickly cleaned it up.

"Oh, my bad y'all, I used to be with the red, now I'm with the blue team. 97.9 THE BEAT!"

Whew.

After my two-hour shift, John had me come into his office. "You did good," he said. "A little rusty, but you held your own. You almost killed yourself in the beginning, but I like the energy." He could hear the habits I'd picked up at K104, but he also saw potential. And just like that, he brought me on as a part-time personality. $10 an hour. Again.

Still, I was back. And this time, it felt different.

A couple months later, John moved on to another market. And

in came Mark McCray, the new Program Director. From day one, I respected Mark. He wasn't just some exec chasing popularity or metrics. He cared about talent. About polish. He was a radio man through and through. And while I wasn't yet great on-air, I was hungry. I was willing to outwork anybody.

That drive didn't always translate though. To some of my coworkers, I came off as arrogant. Just like in A-School during my Navy days, people assumed I thought I was better than everybody. I get it—I was confident. I had the streets on lock. I was scorching in the clubs. I pulled up in a wrapped truck with my name on it. My flyer game was elite. I had one that said, "Kayotik Weekends on 97.9 The Beat," and I barely had three shifts a month. But that's how I moved. I was always branding. Always marketing. Always hustling.

But here's what they didn't see.

They didn't see the stress of raising a newborn daughter. Jewel was born May 7, 2011. She was still a baby when I got hired at 97.9 that October. Then Jayla was born March 6, 2013. That made two daughters and one teenage son. Dante was fourteen and eating everything in sight. I had a family now, and $10 an hour wasn't cutting it. I was only working weekends and the occasional fill-in. That meant maybe 16 hours a week, if I was lucky. That paycheck was barely a couple hundred dollars—before taxes.

So, I had to grind elsewhere.

I was still in the clubs, but the strip club hustle wasn't what it used to be. Beamers had shut down in late 2012. My brand was hot, but my income was inconsistent. I still had a nanny. Still had a wife and kids to provide for. But it was getting real.

Every morning I woke up and asked myself: how the hell am I gonna make this work?

Because my kids didn't know about the stress. They just knew they had lunch, toys, and love. And that was never going to change.

I knew I couldn't keep relying on the clubs alone to make ends meet. My family couldn't eat off hype. And it was becoming increasingly difficult to pay the rent, cover bills, and still show up like everything was good. But I always told myself, If things ever got really bad, I could always work at the Post Office.

That was my mental fallback plan. As a Navy vet, I'd get preferential hiring with government jobs. It wasn't glamorous, but it was steady. It was security.

So I did it.

I got a job at the Post Office. And to be real, that shit broke me in ways the club never could.

After everything I had accomplished—radio, clubs, brand work, my name in lights—I was back at the bottom. Temp-to-perm. No guaranteed hours. No benefits. No route. No official vehicle. Just me showing up, hoping to get assigned somewhere.

DJ Kayotik might've been "that guy" in the streets, but to them, I was just Kareem Thomson, the new guy. They treated me like I didn't matter. Like I was just another temp body with no rank, no story, no value. They didn't give a damn about the resume or who I was outside those walls.

That was one of the most humbling chapters of my life.

But I still showed up.

Every. Single. Day.

Even when it was cold. Even when I had to sort and load mail with sore hands. Even when I had to swallow my pride and park my own truck in the back. That same truck that used to be wrapped in my face. The one people recognized me in. I took the wrap off out of embarrassment, but people still knew. That was Kayotik.

Still, I kept saying to myself, My kids will never feel what I felt growing up. They would never go without. Not on my watch.

Then it got worse.

They ran out of government vehicles one day. My supervisor told me, "You can either go home or use your personal vehicle to deliver." My personal vehicle. I looked at him and thought to myself: You want me to deliver mail in the same truck I used to host concerts in? The one everybody knows?

Go home… and do what? Sit in shame because my ego couldn't handle the moment? Hell no. Ain't no goin' home. I had a wife. I had kids. I had responsibilities.

So I said okay. And I hit that route.

I'll never forget it.

I was in Allen, Texas—about 40 minutes north of Dallas— delivering packages in a neighborhood when it happened.

A guy in his driveway looked up at me. Confused. Curious. "DJ Kayotik?" he asked.

I paused for a second. "Yeah, what's up?"

He shook his head, damn near squinting at the disbelief. "Damn… they must not be paying y'all out there. You working for the Post Office?"

That one hit different.

I gave a tight smile, nodded, and kept it moving. But that shit stung. Because he didn't say it to clown me—he said it with real concern. Like, Damn, what happened to you, bro?

Truth is, I had been asking myself that same question every day.

When I got back in the truck, I didn't cry. But I sat there in silence for a long time. That silence turned into a prayer.

God, if this is where you want me to be, I'll stay. But if you've got more for me… I'm ready.

And that next move came quick.

I knew I couldn't let that moment define me. I had too much purpose in me. Too much passion. Too much left to give. So I walked into Mark McCray's office—my Program Director at 97.9—and laid it all out.

I told him everything.

The Post Office. The pain. The frustration. The grind. The embarrassment. The feeling of being overlooked. I told him I had a family to feed. That I didn't know how much longer I could keep doing both, but I couldn't give up. I shed tears in that office. I showed him the real Kareem. The man behind the voice. Behind the mic. Behind the branding.

That moment changed everything.

Mark looked me in my eyes and said, "You've always come off like you had it all together. But we all need somebody. And I see how bad you want it."

God's timing is everything.

Just a few weeks later, a brand-new format was about to hit Dallas: a station called Boom 94.5, focused on classic hip hop. Mark was tapped to lead the morning show along with DJ Menace, who had been the morning show producer at 97.9. That left a spot open… and Mark gave me that shot.

I became the new producer for the nationally syndicated Rickey Smiley Morning Show.

$10 an hour turned into $45,000 a year.

From the bottom. From the truck. From the embarrassment. To a producer role on one of the biggest morning shows in the country. I wasn't just pressing buttons—I was on the mic. Reading traffic. Doing local breaks. Saying my name to the world.

"DJ Kayotik, 97.9 The Beat…"

That was GOD.

Producing for Rickey Smiley was bigger than just a job—it was a breakthrough. For the first time in a long time, I could breathe. I wasn't just hustling to survive, I was finally back in position to thrive. The morning show had a massive audience, and every time they heard my voice, it was another confirmation that I was walking in purpose.

But let's be clear—this wasn't just about a paycheck. This was about positioning. About faith. About legacy.

I had gone from living in my truck, delivering mail in a wrapped SUV, to being on a syndicated morning show aired in over 60 markets. I was no longer chasing moments—I was making impact.

And that impact was something I could finally bring full circle.

See, when I had to give up the name "Mr. Hpnotik," it hurt at first. That name meant something to me. It was a part of my identity. But sometimes, what you think you need is just preparation for what you're really meant to carry.

When Hpnotiq sent the cease-and-desist, I knew it was time for something bigger—something that couldn't be trademarked by a liquor brand. So I called the person I trusted the most: Moms.

I told her I needed a new name—something powerful. Something meaningful. And without hesitation, she said: "What about Kayotik?"

She explained that it represented the energy I brought to every space—the chaos I stirred in the clubs, the way I moved the crowd. But she also gave it purpose. She said if I was serious about building a brand that could evolve and give back, I'd need to attach meaning to the name.

So I turned it into an acronym:

K.A.Y.O.T.I.K. – Kareem's Alternative Youth Options To Improve Kids.

That moment planted the seed for what would eventually become The Kayotik Foundation—my nonprofit for mentoring youth, supporting mental health initiatives, and showing young men that they don't have to follow the same path I did to find greatness. They could find purpose without pain.

And I had Moms to thank for that. Again.

She had given me my identity twice—once as a newborn, and again as a reborn man with purpose.

But the real reason I pushed so hard in all of this? Dante.

I never wanted my son to feel what I felt growing up. I didn't want him to think that success came without struggle, or that manhood meant ego, or that fatherhood was conditional.

I was trying to build something that he could be proud of. Something that could be passed down. A name that would live on even after I was gone.

And then… my phone rang.

It was Nikita.

Everything in my body froze.

CHAPTER 11
"THEY FOUND HIM…"

I answered the phone the second I saw it ring. It felt like I had been waiting for hours for Nikita to call with an update on Dante's whereabouts. In reality, it had only been a little over an hour since we got in the car. Either way, we were finally back on the phone, and I was ready to hear everything. Was he still at the lake? Was he okay? Where do I go? How do I get to him?

But instead, Nikita said three words I'll never forget:

"They. Found. Him."

From the tone of her voice, I knew. Dante was gone.

She didn't have to say anything else. In that instant, my entire world collapsed. The phone went silent. The world went silent. The tears started falling, and as soon as Vanessa saw my face, she knew too. We both broke down. I remember her saying over and over, "I don't understand! I don't understand! How?" All I could manage to say through the sobs was, "My son is gone…"

The rest of the drive was a blur of screaming, crying, and disbelief. My son was gone.

How is it even possible that I was heading to East Texas—not for my son's birthday, not to celebrate a new DJ gig, not to surprise him for the weekend—but because he was no longer with us? Not because I missed him and wanted to hug him, but because he had died. I was in shock. Looking out the window in a daze, thinking of how many times I should've made this drive and didn't. I should've made this drive a thousand times before. Never in my life did I imagine I would be making this drive just to say goodbye.

Nikita gave us directions to the lake as best she could. Her voice was shaking, her spirit was shattered. Her only son was gone—how does a mother wrap her mind around that? I sat in silence, numb, every nerve in my body twisted in pain and rage. Screaming. Crying. Trembling. Every emotion imaginable rushed through me—grief, heartbreak, guilt, fury. You spend your whole life fighting to be better, trying to stay on the right path, doing everything in your power not to be like the father who failed you... and then what? To lose your son right after his 18th birthday?

Why Dante?

Why not me?

Dante was my only son. My firstborn. My legacy.

I couldn't fully accept it until we got to that lake. I needed to see something, anything, to make sense of what Nikita had just told me.

When we arrived, Nikita was already there. But Dante wasn't. The authorities had already taken his body to the morgue.

His best friend and cousins were there, visibly traumatized. They were the last ones to see him alive. I could see the heartbreak and confusion all over their faces.

Dante had gone to the lake with his best friend and his cousins. Nikita didn't even know he was there. But he was 18—had a car, a little freedom, and all the confidence in the world. Plus, Dante was a great swimmer. To him and his crew, it was just another chill Saturday. A regular weekend hangout.

But when he jumped in the lake, everything changed.

He hit his head on a rock. There was a gash on his head—but it didn't seem serious at first. Then his friend and cousins noticed he looked disoriented.

Charles, his best friend, was already in the water. As soon as he realized there were rocks, he tried to wave Dante off from jumping. He screamed for him not to do it. But it was too late—Dante was already mid-air with that big, bright smile on his face.

He hit his head again as he landed, and that's when Charles swam toward him. He grabbed Dante immediately and tried to pull him to safety. But the current was too strong. He couldn't hold on.

And that's when Nikita made the first call.

I don't remember what Charles or Dante's cousins Jasmine and Brad said to me that day. I know they tried to console us. But they were broken, too. The police were there. The entire scene was surreal. My mind was in a fog. All I could do was stare at that water— where my son was last seen alive. Stare at that overpass. Stare at the ripples on the surface, and wonder if that smile on Dante's face was the last thing his friend saw before everything went wrong.

I couldn't move. I couldn't think.

I just kept crying.

But more than anything—I needed to see him.

Seeing my son lying on a slab in the morgue was the hardest moment of my life.

He was soaking wet. The wound on his head was fresh, but it wasn't even that large—just a jagged line that looked like a lightning bolt from his scalp down to his forehead. I just stood there, staring. Touching his hand. Holding him. Praying he would wake up.

"Please, God… let this be a dream."

I wanted to switch places with him so badly. I would've done anything. Anything.

In that room, I saw all the moments I missed replaying like a movie in my mind. His birth. The hospital in East Texas. Celebrating his arrival back at my apartment in Virginia with Bunkin. Holding him for the first time. Hearing him cry over the phone while I was in Atlanta. Rushing to get him from daycare on September 11th.Shooting hoops together in the front yard in DeSoto. Watching him become DJ Kidd. Hearing him say, "Dad, I'm gonna be a Lumberjack."

It all came rushing in.

And right there, in that cold morgue, I saw myself. I saw my guilt. I saw the sacrifices I didn't make. The time I didn't spend. The drives I didn't take. The birthdays I missed. The shows I could've canceled.

And I hated myself for it.

The only time I got to see my son DJ was during the Kayotik Foundation's first-ever Back-to-School Bash—August 23, 2013. We had free food, school supplies, live performances. It was one of my proudest moments as a father and as a man.

I was finally giving back to the city that had given me so much. And my 16-year-old son, my heir, was running the music.

I watched Dante work that controller like a natural. I gave him a few pointers here and there, but truth be told—he didn't need me. He was locked in. I was watching my legacy in action. One of my favorite pictures to this day is from that event: Dante and I, side by side, both doing what we were born to do.

He wasn't just playing music that day. He was stepping into purpose. He was building something that was going to outlive both of us.

Dante was so serious about being a DJ. He had already started reaching out to local legends like DJ Don Perryon. At the time, Don was killing the college and club scene across East Texas and Dallas. So it made sense that Dante would want to shadow someone like that.

One of his first major parties was with Don—January 17, 2015. It was hyped as "the most anticipated college party of 2015." My son was still in high school and already getting booked alongside top-tier DJs.

Then, just a week later, he rocked another party—this time in Nacogdoches, home of Stephen F. Austin State University. He was spinning for college students at a school he hadn't even started attending yet. DJ Kidd was going to run that campus. No doubt in my mind.

He had written out his goals in his phone—January 4, 2015:

Take SFA over when I get there.

Be in the conversation of one of the hottest DJs in Texas.

Stop being labeled as an opening DJ since I'm a youngin.

Invade UNT for a party.

Get into the EDM world.

Create bigger & better opportunities for myself like maybe tours.

My son wasn't dreaming—he was documenting destiny.

For his 18th birthday, all Dante wanted to do was go to the strip club. That was it. Just hang with his old man.

We planned to go that weekend. His birthday fell on a Sunday— March 8—and he was finally of age. I had a few connections and planned to get him in with no problem. It was nothing for Dante to hop in "Clifford"—his big red Chevy Silverado—and drive to Dallas.

But that weekend, Dallas was hit with a torrential downpour. Streets were flooded. I told him to stay put. "Let's play it safe."

I figured we'd reschedule for next weekend.

We never got that weekend.

That storm may have kept him safe on the road... but it took away the last time I would ever get to celebrate a birthday with my son.

It felt like I stood over Dante's body in that morgue for 24 hours.

I remember feeling like none of it was real. Like I was outside of my own body, watching a nightmare unfold from somewhere above. All I could do was cry. Cry and be angry. Cry and scream. Cry and wish with everything in me that I could change places with him.

I hugged him over and over again, kissed his cheek... and when I did, water poured from his mouth.

That moment shattered me.

That one image—my son's lifeless body releasing the lake water he drowned in—broke something inside of me I don't think will ever be fixed. That trauma lives in me to this day. The way his clothes clung to him. The small gash on his head that looked like a lightning bolt from his scalp to his brow. The chill of his skin. The silence in the room. I'd give up everything I've ever accomplished for one more second with him.

I kept asking myself the same impossible questions:

Was he conscious when the current pulled him under?

Did he feel it happening?

Was he scared?

Was it quick… or did he suffer?

Those questions haunted me. Still do. But the reality was brutal and unchangeable: nothing would bring my son back. Not my prayers. Not my screams. Not my tears.

Nothing.

Eventually, the staff at the mortuary asked us to leave. But how could I? How do you just walk away from your child and leave them in a cold room with strangers who don't know their laugh, their smell, their story? They didn't know Dante. They didn't know DJ Kidd. They hadn't seen him DJ his first big party, or heard him talk about taking over the EDM world. They didn't know his goals. They didn't know his heart.

They had a job to do. I understood that. But I didn't want to leave him. Ever.

They had to physically pull me away.

After we left the mortuary, we went back to Nikita's house. It was full. Packed with family. Friends. People trying to process what just happened. People trying to console us. I sat in Dante's room, looking at his pictures, his shoes, his DJ equipment—anything that still held a trace of him.

And all I could think was how much light he brought into my life… and how much went out when he left.

On April 4, 2015, I didn't just lose my son.

I lost everything. My heartbeat. My reason. My rhythm.

My hustle died that day. My ambition died. My belief in fairness, in justice, in timing—dead.

All I could do was breathe in pain and exhale rage.

We sat in that house for hours.

People were talking—saying things I'm sure were meant to bring comfort—but I couldn't tell you what any of them said. My mind was gone. My spirit was fractured beyond recognition. I sat in Dante's room trying to find pieces of him that I could hold on to. Something. Anything.

Why didn't he tell Nikita he was going to the lake?

Why did he jump in that exact spot?

Why wasn't I there?

I know it was an accident, but fathers always think they can protect. I kept thinking, If I had just been there... maybe I could've changed the outcome. Maybe he'd still be here.

But I wasn't there. And I'll never stop blaming myself for that.

The next morning was Easter Sunday. A day that's supposed to be about resurrection and renewal. But I didn't feel any of that. The only thing I felt was broken. I needed something—anything—to help me make sense of the nightmare I was living.

So, I went to church.

I attended International Body of Christ Church, or IBOC. My homegirl DC Cole worked there, and I had a personal relationship with the pastor, Rickie G. Rush. I had even worked with him when he had a segment on Flava TV. When I walked in, the topic of his sermon hit me like a punch to the chest:

"How things in life can change suddenly."

Suddenly. That word cut straight through me.

I just sat there in the pew and cried.

Then Pastor said something else I'll never forget:

"This might be your first service without your loved one."

I broke all the way down. There was no controlling it. I cried like a child. I had no armor left.

After service, he met with me privately in his chambers. I told him what had happened—that I had lost my son the day before. His face dropped. He hugged me and held on tight.

"Kareem," he said, "I'm going to be your cornerman. Whatever you need. You're in the fight of your life now, and I'll be in your corner."

Then he said something that both broke me and lifted me:

"I'm going to tell you something that's not going to feel good. God sometimes allows you to go through the hardest moments of your life to bring you closer to Him. Dante's job was done. Yours isn't. God needs you now."

I didn't want to hear that. But somehow, I knew he was right.

Even stranger, Nikita told me Dante had been asking his friends questions days before the accident—eerie questions.

"How many people do you think would show up to my funeral?"

He'd asked her that more than once. I think his spirit knew something was coming. I think God was preparing him. Preparing us. I don't know what you believe, but I know what I felt.

That moment with Pastor Rush replays in my head constantly. His words became a lifeline. Without God, without faith, without that truth—I don't know if I would've survived.

Without relying on my faith, without trusting God, without staying prayerful—I would not be standing here today. This book wouldn't exist. I wouldn't be here to tell you Dante's story. I wouldn't have found a way to keep breathing.

That day, I recommitted my life to God. I had nothing left. No strength. No answers. No plan. I felt like an empty shell: of a man, of a husband, of a father. That feeling stayed with me for years. Still lingers at times.

Even now, I sometimes feel like a failure. A failure as a father. A failure as a protector. A failure as a man. People say things like "make him proud," and I try. Every day, I try. I live to make my son proud. I write to honor his memory. I serve to turn my pain into purpose.

I'm still grieving. Still learning how to carry the weight of loss. Still trying to turn something this devastating into something meaningful. This book is a part of that process. Not a conclusion— just a chapter. A chapter for every parent out there who's lost a child. For anyone who's walked through grief and tried to keep walking.

This is me, saying it's okay to still hurt.

It's okay to not have moved on.

It's okay to find purpose in pain, even if the pain never fully goes away.

The truth is, it won't go away. Not completely. But it can be redirected. It can be used. It can light the way for others.

And speaking of light...

I'll never forget the first DJ name my mom suggested for Dante. Before he was DJ Kidd, she wanted to call him DJ Light—based on Matthew 5:16:

"In the same way, let your light shine before others, that they may see your good deeds and glorify your Father in heaven."

My son's light still shines. In me. In Vanessa. In Jewel and Jayla. In Nikita. In every life he touched. In every person who hears his story.

His light didn't go out. It just rose higher.

And if giving it to God brings me closer to Him and to Dante...

Then there's no other way I'd want to live.

CHAPTER 12
"SEE YOU AGAIN..."

Dante was buried in a gold casket. The top was glass and fully see-through. Nikita picked it out. My Moms always told my son he was a prince, and his funeral service was definitely fit for royalty. Even down to the velvet ropes that kept people from touching the casket. A fully see-through casket from head to toe wasn't common, but it was what he deserved. We didn't want anyone smudging it, so the funeral home roped off the section. Dante was basically in VIP— as he should be. Just like he would've been in a few more years.

Most of the details of his wake and funeral came from his godmother, Brandice. To be honest, it's all a blur for me. Was I there? Of course. But do you think I remember the specifics from the darkest moment of my life? It's painful enough to relive the moments I do remember. Thankfully, Dante was surrounded by angels on Earth like Brandice, who could recall what my memory has blacked out. She and Nikita's mom handled nearly all the arrangements. Because truthfully, neither Nikita nor I were in any kind of mental space to make those decisions. That being said, I'll try to tell you about Dante's wake and homegoing service.

But first—I need to tell you about where our relationship stood before the accident. There had been a rift between Dante and me after I married Vanessa. She stayed on me about fixing it. It took maybe a little over a year, but I finally grew up and did what needed to be done. We got back to being close again. By 2011, our bond was tighter than ever.

That year, Dante had to undergo extensive surgery. He was only 14, but already a beast—he played every sport. When he and Nikita first moved back to East Texas, he jumped into football. That Christmas, Moms was in town—as she always was—and she and Dante were playing a boxing game on the Nintendo Wii. As she joked about him whooping on his grandma, she noticed a lump protruding from his back. When she asked him about it, Dante said he hadn't even noticed. Moms immediately brought it to our attention and stayed on Nikita until she took him to the doctor.

Turns out, he had scoliosis. The prognosis meant he'd be pulled from football for a long time—maybe even for good. It was devastating for him, but catching it early was a blessing. The doctors said if it had gone another year, the damage would've been permanent.

Nikita brought him to Dallas for treatment at Scottish Rite Hospital. The surgery lasted six to eight hours. I was there for every single moment. It was hard seeing my son in that condition. I'll never forget the moment when he was high off morphine, flirting with the nurses. We laughed, but behind the smiles, I was terrified. He had rods placed in his back. His football dreams were done. But he eventually bounced back and moved on to basketball and track.

Part of his recovery included learning how to walk again. And besides the nurses helping him, his daddy helped him. I remember walking him down the halls, his arms wrapped around my shoulders as he slowly relearned how to move. I was there—literally every step of the way.

That moment solidified our bond.

Years later, the Kayotik Foundation put on a Christmas event and donated toys to Scottish Rite. I give them all the credit for saving my son's future. That hospital held a special place in our hearts.

Before Dante's wake, there was a balloon release in Cason, Texas—just a few miles from Nikita's house. Maybe 300 people came out to celebrate my son's life. And then came the most traumatic two days of my life.

Dante had been scheduled to attend three proms his senior year. We buried him in the white blazer he wore to one of them. He was also dressed in one of his favorite shirts—a red and white plaid Ralph Lauren button-down—and a new pair of Revival Jeans he had just gotten a few weeks prior. That was his favorite brand. He'd wanted a Ferragamo belt for prom, and I made sure he had it for his service. The night before his accident, he stayed up all night waiting on the release of a new pair of red and white Jordans. They completed the outfit he'd picked out. That was the last thing he wore.

His wake was held on April 10, 2015—six days after his accident. But I couldn't tell you how I was feeling. I was there, but I wasn't present. Just a shell of a man, walking through the darkest moment of his life. I know DC Cole drove a transportation van for the family. My Moms, stepdad, cousins, and aunts flew down from New York. Vanessa and her mom drove separately. I don't remember why. But I do remember being distant. Distant from everything and everyone, including Vanessa. I didn't care about anything or anyone. Not even myself. My mindset was: I gotta deal with this pain on my own.

Still, I tried to be strong for others—whatever that looked like. But how do you console people who are feeling the same pain you are? You don't. You just exist. You show up. You break inside quietly. That's what I did.

What I do remember, though, was seeing my son lying there. Seeing his friends. Thanking them for coming. And hearing "See You Again" by Wiz Khalifa and Charlie Puth play on repeat for five hours. That song was from Furious 7, the same movie Dante was supposed to go see the day he passed. His friends used it in a video collage of memories. It became the soundtrack of his homegoing. That slideshow looped during the entire wake. And every time it played, that hook hit me again:

"It's been a long day…without you, my friend."

Dante's friends shared stories about him. One story from his best friend Jesse stood out. Jesse said he was being teased at school for not having nice sneakers. And Dante—without hesitation—took the shoes off his own feet and gave them to him. I broke down right then and there.

As a parent, you try to instill values in your children. You hope they stick. But to hear that story? To know your son saw his friend in need and gave him the shoes off his feet? That meant everything. He didn't just grow up with material blessings—he grew up with a heart. And he used it.

Dante wasn't just the cool, popular kid. He wasn't just an athlete or a DJ. He was a giver. Without having to experience hunger or struggle the way I did growing up, he still had empathy for others. And he acted on it.

The next day was the day.

"Celebrating the Life and Legacy of Dante Akee Thomson."

He used to ask his mom how many people she thought would show up to his funeral. The answer? Over 1,000 people.

His obituary said he "grew up surrounded by an immeasurable love." And that was the absolute truth. The service itself was beautiful. I'm truly thankful to JC White Funeral & Cremation Services for how they handled every detail—with both structure and sympathy. The owner, JC, was actually close friends with Nikita, so he came to the house personally to make arrangements. They did an amazing job.

Jewel had seen Jesse—Dante's best friend—and thought it was her big brother. They resembled each other. She was only three, almost four years old at the time. And she and Dante were very close. She might've been too young to fully understand death, but she was smart enough to know something wasn't right. She saw how sad everyone was and didn't even want to go inside the church. She definitely wasn't the only one who didn't want to face what was coming.

There was a huge floral arrangement draped over Dante's casket—red roses with white accents. Brandice got those. Hibbett Sports sent a large flower arrangement as well. Dante was always up in there buying shoes or waiting overnight for the Jordan releases. There were also two tall easels on either side of his casket with large photos of him. One was a 7-foot poster from an event he DJ'd with Yung Nation. I think Nikita still has it.

His casket was opened for immediate family. We tucked him in ourselves—pulled the blanket up and laid it over him. I don't even know how I got through that moment. I was still in disbelief. I couldn't fully process what I was seeing. My son—dressed in the outfit he had planned for prom—now lying there forever still. Even then, reality hadn't hit me.

I spoke at the funeral.

At least I'm told I did.

Brandice said I spoke beautifully. She said I thanked everyone for being there, talked about our relationship, what it meant to be Dante's father. I vaguely remember writing something out beforehand. I think I even ended with a poem. Something I found online that felt like it was written just for me. For him. It read like Dante was speaking from heaven, letting us know he was okay. It felt like he sent that poem to me. I remember thinking: This is what he would want me to say.

I also wrote my own poem. It's in the obituary. I only remember it because I've seen it so many times since. I ended with these lines:

"I miss you more than words could say.

With you again I will be someday.

So until that time shall come,

Remember I love you so very much, son."

The slideshow played again during the service. And that same song, "See You Again," echoed through the sanctuary.

"We've come a long way from where we began...

Oh I'll tell you all about it when I see you again."

I stayed at the gravesite until his casket was fully covered.

Just like at the mortuary, I didn't want to leave him alone.

How do you bury your child and walk away like it's normal?

I don't even remember leaving the cemetery. Brandice told me I was late to the repast because I refused to go. I believe it. I remember Vanessa trying to make me eat. I didn't touch a thing. Couldn't eat. Couldn't sleep. Couldn't think.

At the repast, my cousin Caryn gave me dog tags with Dante's image on them. What she didn't know was that I had buried my only set of military dog tags with my grandfather. Those new dog tags became my lifeline. My armor. I wore them daily for over a year until they tarnished. I still have them. I always will.

Dante graduated from Pittsburg High School on May 29, 2015.

While he wasn't there physically, his school made sure he was present in spirit. They placed a single flower in his seat. When his name was called, the auditorium fell silent. Then they presented his honorary diploma with reverence and respect.

The Pittsburg Independent School District even donated a magnolia tree in his memory. They planted it on the side of the high school, with a plaque that bears his name. His legacy would live on in that soil. That plaque. That tree.

His red Chevy Silverado—"Big Red", or "Clifford," as he called it—is still parked at Nikita's house. It still runs. Still has the 24-inch rims he saved up for. Nikita and her father still drive it sometimes. She didn't want to keep the clothes he drowned in, but one of the rescue team members gave her the white blanket they wrapped him in. It's folded up in the truck, along with one of his favorite t-shirts. And for a long time, that truck smelled like the lake.

In the weeks and months that followed, I was emotionally and spiritually empty. There's no blueprint for grief like that. There's no playbook for burying your child and continuing to function. But Dario and CJ, the owner and general manager of Park Ave, did something I'll never forget. They gave me paid time off from the club. That's unheard of. DJs don't get paid unless they show up. But they wanted me to take all the time I needed to grieve and heal. I think I took a month and a half.

Nikita organized a 5K walk in East Texas called Team LLTK – Long Live The Kidd. The team won two awards: Most People on a Team and Best Designed T-shirt. The turnout was beautiful.

But I didn't go.

I stayed in the house and did absolutely nothing. I was paralyzed by pain. The only thing I did consistently was go to work at 97.9 The Beat. Tami, the GM at the time, offered me time off too. But I needed something to distract me during the day. Just a few hours of structure. So I told myself, I can at least do these four hours. That's all I had in me.

I was back on the air the Monday after Dante's funeral. And I cried every single morning.

Rickey Smiley showed me so much love and support during that time. He knew what it felt like to endure tragedy and still have to perform. He would check in. Embrace me. Cover me in prayer. He was one of the few people who could make me smile, even while I was breaking inside. I'm forever grateful to him.

Even my daughter Jewel was affected in ways that would take years to surface. She was still so young when Dante passed—only 3 years old—but she felt the shift. She saw the sadness. She saw the silence. She saw Clifford parked in the driveway without her big brother behind the wheel.

Eventually, Vanessa and I had to explain what death meant. We had to tell her the truth. A few years later, she was in East Texas with Brandice and said something that shattered all of us.

She said,

"I want to hit my head so I can go in the sky and see my brother."

She thought that's how you got to heaven—by having an accident. Brandice sat her down and explained gently,

"Your brother had an accident, but he's always with you. He loves you, and when you miss him, look up in the sky and thank God for him."

Brandice was Dante's godmother. She and Nikita are also Jewel and Jayla's godmothers. That's our blended family. People may not understand how a wife, an ex-girlfriend, and children from different relationships can all remain close. But Dante brought us together. He created a family bond that can never be broken. His spirit is in every one of us.

CHAPTER 13
"THERAPY DIDN'T FIX ME..."

Everyone checks on you after something tragic happens. And I'll forever be grateful for the calls, texts, and drop-ins. But eventually, the calls stop. The texts slow down. And in a lot of ways, that's when the real grieving begins. My birthday is April 26—just a couple weeks after I laid my son to rest. What was anyone supposed to say to me? "Happy birthday, I hope you enjoy it—even though you just buried your son earlier this month"? That kind of message would've either gone unanswered or earned somebody a cuss-out. And with the state I was in, it could've gone either way.

Nikita and I checked in on each other every day. But really, what could we say? There was no comfort. I felt alone. Actually, more than alone—I felt angry. Don't tell me it's gonna be okay. How would you know? When's the last time you lost a child? Just like I used to tell Vanessa when it came to growing up in the hood—don't tell me how to feel unless you've lived it. If you haven't experienced it, you can't tell me it'll get better.

In a strange way, people who followed me on social media were grieving with me. Before Dante passed, I was barely even on Instagram. Honestly, I kind of despised social media. But Dante, like most young people, always told me I should post more. And once he was gone, I started posting as a way to talk to him. I'd share inspirational quotes and prayers like I was writing directly to my son—trying to let him know how much I missed him, how deep the pain was, how bad I needed him.

I'm forever grateful to whoever sent me the information for group therapy. I honestly don't remember who it was—maybe a cousin, a family friend. I just know someone saw my pain and thought enough of me to send the details for an organization called Compassionate Friends.

The first few visits I went alone. That was by choice. I was deep in a selfish space—completely disconnected from everyone I loved. At that time, it was all about Kareem. What I needed. What I was going through. Nobody else could possibly understand. You're not me. You didn't lose my son. You could never understand this kind of pain.

Looking back, I was oblivious—and honestly, indifferent—to the pain the people around me were feeling. My cornerman—my pastor—was praying for me. My superhero—my Moms—was checking in constantly. Vanessa? She was praying for me every single day, even though I was emotionally gone. I was just trying to trust God, but the weight of my grief made me feel like I was the only one in the world suffering. I was angry with everybody. Sick with sorrow. Eating junk food like it was medicine—but it was really just self-destruction.

What drew me to Compassionate Friends was that it was built for people like me. It's a nonprofit created for parents who've lost a child or children—offering understanding, support, and a sliver of hope during the most unnatural pain a parent can endure. I was self-aware enough to know I needed something—anything—that could show me how to grieve without losing myself completely.

Group therapy was harder than I expected. The first session was all introductions. We released balloons in memory of our children. By the third session, I invited Vanessa. She had already been feeling hurt that I started this journey without her. And to be honest, she was right. I hadn't acknowledged her grief at all. I was so wrapped in my own pain, I didn't have space for anyone else's. Still, we started going together a couple times a week.

Compassionate Friends does amazing work—but those sessions were heavy. Every week, you're the new guy with fresh trauma. Then the next week, someone else walks in—also fresh from devastation.

Some people had lost their children ten, even twenty years ago. Others had just buried their baby the week before. Every meeting brought a new horror story, a new layer of grief to carry. And even though I knew it was group therapy, I hadn't realized how each session would reintroduce me to my own pain—over and over again.

Trying to sort through my own feelings while also absorbing the weight of other people's grief... it became too much. After a couple months, Vanessa and I stopped attending. The heaviness lingered long after the meetings ended. We had to walk away.

Grief didn't just weigh heavy on my spirit—it suffocated my marriage. The only thing I could still bring myself to do was show up at the radio station to produce the Rickey Smiley Morning Show. And honestly, I only did that because I needed something to distract me for a few hours. But every single day was a war. I'd get in the car, take the long way down Preston Road, pull over somewhere quiet, and just cry. Ten, fifteen minutes of full-on breakdown before dragging myself through a four-hour shift. If Wiz Khalifa's "See You Again" came on the radio? That was it. I'd be done. I'd pull over and let it all out. That song hit too close. Every time.

When I tell you I didn't care about anyone or anything, that included myself. My health went to hell. Monday through Friday, it was the same toxic routine: I'd leave the station at 9 a.m., hit Chick-Fil-A for waffle fries and a milkshake, then slide straight to Popeyes for a 3-piece with red beans and rice, dirty rice, two biscuits, and a strawberry Fanta. Every. Single. Day. Sometimes six days a week. That was my coping mechanism. No gym. No prayer. No self-control. Just food. And grief.

I went from a lean 180 to a sluggish, medically obese 240 pounds. My doctor looked at my labs and told me my cholesterol was through the roof. I nodded and walked out. I didn't care. Nothing in me cared. Because the one person who would've pushed me to eat better, move more, take care of myself—he was gone. So, what was the point?

At home, things weren't much better. The woman I had searched for half my life—the woman I eloped with just to never lose again— was now a stranger in her own house. I barely spoke to Vanessa.

Didn't reach for her. Didn't check on her. She was grieving too, but I didn't see that. Or maybe I just didn't want to.

Sometimes, I'd sit in the backyard for hours and cry. Other times, I'd just hop in the car and drive—no destination, no explanation, no phone call. I barely interacted with my daughters. I didn't know how to. I had become so emotionally unavailable that the only moments Jayla and Jewel got with me were the ones Vanessa forced.

Rightfully so—she was doing everything in her power to keep me tethered to our kids, to life, to reality. But I wasn't having it. I resisted her love. I rejected her help. And little by little, that pain didn't just sit in the room—it became the room. It filled every inch of our home. And Vanessa? She was drowning in it, too. She was growing tired of living in a house with a ghost.

The grief had completely swallowed me. And I was pulling everyone I loved down with me.

But the weight of grief didn't stop at silence or distance. It dug even deeper. What started as isolation soon turned into something darker—something far more dangerous than just shutting people out.

While I never considered leaving my marriage, I did consider leaving the earth. My life didn't matter to me. Outside of losing my son, nothing mattered to me. My only consideration of my wife and daughters was that I had life insurance, so I'd at least be leaving them with something. This mentality carried on into the next year, and Vanessa was fed up. She had taken my blatant disregard for her and our children long enough. It wasn't just me being depressed and generally uninterested in life. I wasn't talking to her. Not considering her in any aspect of my life. There were plenty of times where I'd go visit Dante and not even ask if she wanted to come. I'd hop on my bike and go for a ride, no invitation. Not that I didn't care about her. Vanessa Rose is the love of my life!! I just didn't realize how my actions, or lack thereof, was weighing down on her. Vanessa was ready to give up on us, and that was my wake-up call. It was never my goal to push her away, I just didn't know how to invite her in. But there was no way I was going to lose her. I knew I had to fight for my marriage and my kids.

I started therapy with Ms. Wanda in 2015, initially going twice a week. She ripped the band-aid off and didn't hold back any punches. I was thinking that the only issue I was facing was navigating through the loss of my son. But Wanda showed me that I was an extremely traumatized man from childhood to adulthood. There was so much unaddressed trauma from before Dante was even born. I thought I had worked through all my childhood issues and pain. But simply getting older doesn't equate to healing! What I discovered was that burying pain only works for so long.

Wanda put a mirror in front of me and exposed me to myself. I didn't like the Kareem I saw in that mirror. It was challenging to realize everything I thought I was, I wasn't. She helped me understand that I needed to forgive. I needed to learn how to forgive. She brought up my pops and I shrugged it off, told her I had forgiven him and we didn't even need to discuss him. She saw right through that bullshit. I hadn't even started on working to forgive him. From homelessness, the clarinet, fighting my father…buried inside of myself was a traumatized little boy who grew into a man who was completely broken. Layer by layer, Wanda peeled back the covers and showed me how I didn't deal with all my pain, and how much pain I was subconsciously causing because of it. I'm so thankful for Ms. Wanda because she unpacked Kareem Thomson. And Kareem had a lot of baggage.

As someone who prides himself on being selfless, learning how selfishly I had been operating was an eye-opener. The man who was proud that his son gave his best friend the shoes off his feet… was the same man neglecting his family. Wanda knew that losing Dante was obviously a huge issue for me, but she showed me how it was also a big issue for my family—and I didn't even recognize it.

When you're grieving, you're in a space of expecting people to feel the same pain, the same way you do. I expected Vanessa and the girls to be just as sad as I was, and to express that sadness like I did. On the 4th of every month, I posted Dante to my social media. Since he passed on April 4th, it became my monthly anniversary, as well as a painful reminder of that day. I expected my followers to understand why I was posting. I expected people to understand why my phone would be on Do Not Disturb and why I didn't want to be bothered.

Wanda taught me how to understand my grief, stop projecting my feelings onto others, and to lower my expectations of thinking people will feel or understand my pain. Logically speaking—if I'm the only one who lost a son—why would I expect others to respond the way I did?

Until Wanda put that mirror in front of me, I had no idea how extremely self-absorbed I had been. She taught me how to effectively communicate with my wife and kids, and I'm still utilizing those tools today. The most revealing thing to me was how, in some ways, I was just like my father.

Using your hatred for someone as motivation is incredibly damaging. I prided myself on being nothing like my father—meanwhile, I had spent almost a year neglecting my family. The bills were paid, but our house wasn't a home, because after Dante passed, I had put no effort into making it one. We had bought a house six months before Dante's accident. To go from foreclosure in Desoto to homeownership again in Frisco was something to be proud of. But I didn't care.

Wanda showed me how unhealthy it was to live my life to not be like someone—and how that focus can subconsciously turn you into the very thing you were trying to avoid. My motivation was to be nothing like my pops. But that motivation was really just trauma and anger.

Sometimes, I had to be hit to really just go. I thought that only pertained to my martial arts studies. Ms. Wanda showed me how I never healed from life's punches. I just covered the bruises.

Before therapy, I prided myself on being this strong Black man who's been through the fire and made it. You couldn't break me because I had already been broken! I came from the trenches and came out of it with an unbreakable armor. But in reality, I was a hurt, sensitive brother who didn't know how to effectively communicate with his wife and daughters. I really frowned upon being called sensitive. But I learned that it's okay to be aware that you're hurting. Words hurt. Things hurt. Actions hurt. And keeping all that pain inside was only causing me to be distant toward the people who meant the most to me.

I needed to fix my selfish ways to be a productive man, father, husband and friend. She showed me that I wasn't just broken—I was defeated. And related to those hits that life had given me lately? It was okay to cry. Crying didn't make you weak; it was a healthy release. Understanding more about myself revealed the decisions I had made up until that point.

The reason I chased the bag so aggressively today was for all those days I stood outside of Key Foods, hustling for car fare for my Moms. I held the mindset that I would be sure that my family never knew what it was to see an empty refrigerator. While I take great pride in being a provider, that same mentality caused me to miss out on moments with my son. I missed so many opportunities to take that two-and-a-half-hour drive to East Texas to see him. Focused too heavily on being DJ Kayotik instead of Kareem Thomson—the father, the husband.

To be honest, I didn't even realize that I was being selfish. But in hindsight, there are so many instances I can point out.

When Vanessa and I eloped and Dante wasn't happy about it, my response was that he should want to see me happy. I had no regard for how the situation could've made him feel. Now that I was grieving, I didn't even realize that my wife and daughters were also grieving and didn't have the man of the house to lean on.

It's crazy—you can walk around thinking you got your shit together because your money is right, and not realize that so many things you've experienced—and never healed from—may be blocking your real blessings.

One Sunday during church, Pastor Rush was talking about being able to forgive because otherwise, you'll block your blessings. Who knows how many blessings I blocked because I hated my father? There were times I was even mad at my Moms for forgiving him. I carried that hatred into adulthood, and accordingly, I was too damaged to see the lessons in my experiences.

Therapy also taught me that there is no timetable or handbook on processing grief. There are five stages of grief—denial, anger, depression, bargaining, acceptance—but there isn't really anything anyone can teach you about processing it. It just has to be experienced. You can learn ways to work through the stages and understand that those stages aren't in any specific order. I was heavily in the depressed stage, to the point that the VA had to step in. I was having suicidal thoughts, so I had to speak to a psychiatrist.

I didn't exactly want to end my life; I wanted to be closer to my son. So, while there was no date set, I somewhat had a plan. Basically, if I was gonna do it, this is how I would. My "plan" would be to drive to the lake where Dante jumped, drive over the overpass with the windows up and just not get out. I wanted to be strong, but all the fight I had in me was gone.

All the things I had gone through in my life didn't scratch the surface of the pain I felt losing my son. I remember asking God, "why am I even here?" What stopped me from driving over that overpass was thinking about leaving my Moms, my kids, Vanessa, Nikita. And Dante. I thought about how disappointed Dante would be if I gave up. Because of him, I continued to fight.

The psychiatrist at the VA prescribed me antidepressants. While still operating in selfishness, one day I got dressed and told Vanessa I was going to see Dante. No invitation. To be real, even me telling her I was going was progress. But my mindset was I'm doing me. I'm driving by myself to see my son.

I went to see Dante every week or every couple of weeks to place fresh red roses and flowers on his headstone. It was normal for me to cry the entire drive there, while sitting with him, and leaving. But after starting the medication, I was sitting there wanting to cry and I couldn't. It was the worst feeling in the world—to want to release and shed tears while sitting with your son who's six feet under, but the meds have you so messed up that you can't.

I called the doctor immediately and told him I didn't want to take the medication anymore. The doctor suggested they wean me off of it, but I said hell no. I knew I needed a different way to cope with my pain and the pain I was causing my family.

Vanessa and I began marriage counseling with Ms. Wanda as well. She asked the right questions to make me unpack my baggage—even things I thought I had already dealt with. Wanda gave Vanessa and me homework. She helped me see that my wife was grieving as well, and she needed me.

I learned what I meant to my family, as well as what they meant to me. I lost Dante, but I still had two little girls I couldn't abandon. Spending time with my family needed to be my top priority—that's time you can never get back. With Dante, I have to live through pictures. But pictures run out! There were people in my house who needed me, and I needed them.

Through learning to be more transparent, I was able to better communicate with Vanessa. I learned that a lot of times I was perceiving things negatively, which was the complete opposite of what was intended. Ms. Wanda taught me to repeat the message back to them for clarity. A simple "so you're saying that..." helped clear up a lot of miscommunications between Vanessa and me.

I finally found the courage to tell my wife when something hurt me. I began to understand my triggers—not just what sparked the emotion, but the deeper wounds behind it. I learned how to pause, pray, and process instead of shutting down or pushing people away. It's a process I'm still learning, especially as a husband and father, but every step brings me closer to the man God has called me to be.

Therapy helped me develop skillsets to communicate and grieve differently. I learned that every day will be different. One day I might see the light. The next day that light may be dim. The day after, it might be completely dark. We go through cycles, and that's okay. If you've lost someone, take your time in trying to heal.

I say that as a man who's made peace with the fact that I may never heal from losing my son. But part of my healing process is to learn from it, grow from it, and try to help others. But to tell you that I lost my son and ten years later I'm healed? No. I have some good days, some bad days, some mediocre days. I have days when I spiral into depression. The difference is that now, I have the tools to stop me from backsliding into where I used to be.

As Veda Loca would often say to me, "It's okay to not be okay. But it's not okay to stay that way."

We worked with Ms. Wanda for four or five years—going from twice a week, to weekly, to biweekly, then monthly. It wasn't a fast process, and it wasn't perfect. But it was necessary. And it saved me.

Therapy didn't "fix" me. But it helped me learn myself.

I still consider myself depressed, but not in the way that I was before. I'm not down every day, but I certainly have days where I feel myself going into a depression. Thanks to therapy, I'm proactive on those days. I seek God even more. I pour into myself more. I do things that make me happy. I spend more time with the girls. With Vanessa. With the gym.

The gym is my sanctuary. Running is my therapy.

My eating habits had caused my weight to get out of control; I could barely tie my shoes without being out of breath. I was carrying over sixty pounds of pain and sadness on my body, and it showed. Now, my health is my wealth. I go to the gym to clear my mind. To reflect. I look at those old pictures of myself overweight and I remind myself that we can't ever go back to that version. Not physically. Not spiritually. Not emotionally.

I'll post inspirational quotes on social media. It's crazy because people will reach out thanking me, saying my post helped them— when they don't even realize it was more for me than anyone else.

That's the thing about healing. Sometimes you think you're sharing to inspire others, but really, you're just pouring out what you wish someone would've told you. What you wish someone had said to you when you were in your darkest place. And somehow, by helping them, you help yourself.

I can't tell you that I'm happy today. But I'm thankful. I'm blessed. I'm humbled. I'm extremely grateful for the things I've accomplished and the journey I'm currently on.

But do I wake up on any given day and say I'm happy? No. How can I be?

I've had some happy moments. But those moments are like putting a fresh Band-Aid on a wound. Once I remove the Band-Aid, the wound is still open. I still feel its pain. The word "happy" doesn't really exist for me yet. But I have hope that one day it will.

Forgiveness really is more for you than the person you're forgiving. My pastor told me that sometimes God will take something from you in order to move you closer to Him. By 2018, I felt like God was testing me on what I'd learned—checking in to see if I would still give it all to Him.

My mother called to tell me my father had passed. I'm not sure how, but something about his liver being bad. Unfortunately, he could never find a way to leave the streets, and it led to his demise. I was adamant about not attending the funeral. For what? So I respectfully declined when Moms told me about it. She said she'd pray for me and wanted me to pray on the decision.

So I did.

Was this God testing me?

I went to therapy to save my family. I was learning to grow and better communicate. I had an amazing therapist who was teaching me about myself. This decision felt like an open-book test. I had all the answers I needed in the work I'd been doing—the true question was, would I apply the knowledge and finally learn this lesson?

I told Vanessa I wasn't going to the funeral. But having learned how to self-reflect, I sat in front of that proverbial mirror and prayed.

In order for me to grow and not block my blessings, I have to honor him—whether I want to or not.

The Bible says to honor thy mother and father. The best way I could do that was to show my final respects.

I decided to forgive my father at his funeral. And that's when I really felt free.

Free from the hatred I had been harboring for a man who was caught up in the disease of addiction. Whose actions were motivated by something beyond his control. That little boy who waited outside the store for a clarinet that never came was now a man who knew it was okay to mourn the possibilities of what could've been. And he also understood that it was okay to let it go.

I felt that I was making progress with God and growing in the direction He set for me.

Without the motivation of being nothing like my father, I could finally focus on growing closer to my Father in Heaven. To being a better father to Jewel and Jayla—and even Dante—by becoming the best version of myself.

It truly felt like the moment I forgave my dad, blessings began pouring in.

Pastor Rush was right when he said, "You don't realize how much you're blocking your blessings until you forgive someone who's done you wrong." I let it go. I gave it to God. And then God began to give to me.

I stopped focusing on not being like my dad and started focusing on being a man my son would be proud of. I always say Dante is my favorite DJ and my greatest motivation. So I live to make my motivator proud.

Dante's dreams would live through me—in more ways than one.

He wanted to tour. He wanted to rock big crowds. He wanted to be respected. And maybe he didn't get to do it the way he envisioned, but I carry his name and spirit with me every time I step into a booth. Every time I get behind a mic. Every time I tell my story. His name is in my heartbeat.

The Kayotik Foundation became more than a name. It became a purpose. A calling. A mission built not just on my story—but on his. Through LLTK, we've fed families, provided school supplies, poured into youth programs, raised mental health awareness, and reminded people that healing is a journey, not a destination. That it's okay to be in pain, but it's not okay to live there.

Every time I see Jewel or Jayla smile, I see a piece of Dante. Every time I push myself harder at the gym, speak on a panel, show up for a young man who needs guidance—I see a piece of him. And every time someone tells me, "your post helped me," or "your story gave me strength," I know it's because I found the courage to tell the truth about my pain—and the faith to keep going anyway.

It didn't happen overnight. There was no light switch. No magic therapy session. No miracle prayer. Just consistent, committed surrender. I gave God the pieces of my shattered heart, and He handed me purpose. He didn't promise it wouldn't hurt. He didn't say I wouldn't break. But He gave me enough grace to survive it—and enough reason to keep walking in it.

This chapter of my life wasn't written in ink. It was written in tears. In late-night prayers and early morning doubt. In Chick-fil-A parking lots and Popeye's drive-thrus. In bike rides to nowhere. In days I didn't want to wake up. In sessions with Ms. Wanda. In every single moment I thought, "I can't do this," and still chose to try.

I'm still becoming. Still healing. Still growing.

But the difference now is—I know who I am.

I'm a man who's lost everything and gained a deeper understanding of grace.

I'm a father who still visits his son, even if the visits are now made of memories, prayers, and fresh red roses.

I'm a husband who learned how to fight for love, not just because he didn't want to lose it—but because he finally knew how to show up for it.

I'm a man who thought therapy was a fix—and found out it was a mirror.

I'm not "fixed."

I'm faithful.

And I'm finally free.

CHAPTER 14
"50 CENT SAVED MY LIFE…"

After producing the Rickey Smiley Morning Show for a few years, a shift was coming to morning radio in Dallas. In January 2018, Veda Loca was getting her own, well-deserved morning show. She had been holding down afternoons (3–7 PM) on The Beat, and I'd see her a few times a week when she came in early to prep. But with Rickey relocating his show back to Atlanta, the station had to decide: keep Rickey's syndicated show running, or bet on something local. Veda was already the face of the station—a Dallas radio legend—so it only made sense to build a homegrown morning show around her.

But where did that leave me?

I'd heard rumblings about a new morning show coming, but I wasn't hearing my name in those conversations. I think they assumed they could just transition me from producing Rickey's show to producing for Veda. But there were a couple of issues with that. First, Veda liked to run her own board. She didn't need a traditional board op. And second, I didn't want to be just the guy pushing buttons anymore. I'd already done that. I wanted a mic. I wanted to co-host. I wanted more.

So I did what I always do—I advocated for myself.

I had a conversation with our GM, Tami, about the direction of the station and where I saw myself fitting in. I told her I believed in what the new show could be, and I believed I could bring something unique to it. She listened. We talked. And in the end, I became the fourth mic on the brand-new Veda Loca Morning Show.

That moment was full circle. From sending in an audition video, to working street team events, to producing Rickey's nationally syndicated show—now I was part of a local morning show. We had billboards all over the city. Our station vehicle was wrapped with our faces, just like my old Expedition. And for a while, the show was even simulcast on the CW. We were visible. I felt like all the years of grinding were finally beginning to pay off.

The lineup was solid. It was Veda, myself, J Kruz, and Jazzi Black. Kruz came from nights, and he and I had known each other for a while from the club scene. We had a natural rhythm. He was polished, knew how to execute on air, and had real presence. Jazzi, on the other hand, was brand new to radio. She came from the digital team—our station's videographer. They threw her straight into the fire. She was nervous, of course, but her raw talent was obvious. She had that millennial perspective, a fresh voice, and a vibrant energy we didn't even know the show needed. Tami really did her thing assembling that team. And when we launched, we weren't even looking at our direct competition, K104. We had our sights set on the Breakfast Club. That was our real benchmark.

Now here's the twist: I went from Veda pushing me into radio years earlier, to now being her producer—and sometimes the one pushing her. That wasn't always easy. She had been doing solo radio for a long time, so transitioning into an ensemble wasn't second nature to her. We had a bit of a love-hate relationship on the air. Always respectful, but we definitely bumped heads. I was reading her energy every day while also trying to keep the show together, keep the content fresh, and keep my own voice intact. It was a delicate balance. But I'm from Southside Jamaica, Queens—what's a challenge to me?

And I didn't just want to show up. I wanted to grow. I had produced for a national morning show, but producing locally meant something different. It meant helping build the content, sourcing the stories, setting the tone, and creating moments. I wanted to elevate. So when I heard about Morning Show Bootcamp—a national radio conference filled with workshops and networking opportunities—I knew I had to be there.

The last time I'd been to Chicago was back in my corporate days—Project Manager Kareem. I was there for some PepsiCo conference or meeting, nothing exciting. I didn't have much free time, but I managed to swing by the Sears Tower and, of course, try some pizza. Chicago folks swear by their deep dish, but let me be clear—New York pizza is still king. Don't argue me on that.

This time around, though, I wasn't there in a corporate suit. I was DJ Kayotik, morning show producer, flying in to sharpen my craft. Morning Show Bootcamp was packed with radio professionals from all over—big personalities, up-and-comers, producers, consultants. It was energizing just being around people passionate about the same hustle. I wanted to soak up game and come back to Dallas with new ideas, new skills, and a bigger vision for what we could do with the show.

But I also knew that 50 was in town.

Word was he was in Chicago filming Power Book IV: Force, the spinoff centered around Tommy's character. I wasn't sure how long he'd be there, but I hit up some of my promoter friends who told me there was an exclusive industry event going on that weekend, and some of the Power cast would be in attendance. I figured there was a chance 50 might show up. I wasn't banking on it. I just thought, if the stars align, I'll slide through.

Sure enough, I pull up to the event, and 50 is in VIP upstairs.

My guys got me past the promoters, and then I had to get past 50's security. I stepped to the rope, and the moment 50 spotted me, he flagged me through. Just like that. Security stepped aside, and there I was—face-to-face with Boo Boo from the block, now global superstar Curtis "50 Cent" Jackson.

We smiled, dapped up, hugged. The first thing I said was, "Yo, I'm so fucking proud of you, bro!" He laughed, shook his head like, "Man, you here?" Then he asked what I was doing these days. I told him I was in radio now, producing a morning show, and was in town for Bootcamp.

He grinned. "I can't believe Reem is on radio."

We stood there vibing, talking, reminiscing. Nothing Hollywood about it. Just two Southside kids from Jamaica, Queens, catching up in a Chicago VIP. I told him I'd catch him later, gave him his space, and dipped out. What I didn't realize at the time was... I wasn't just reconnecting with an old friend.

I was reconnecting with my future.

Fast forward to 2019.

My phone rang, and it was Rene Castillo—one of the music managers tied to 50's brand. We'd known each other from back in the day when DJs built real relationships with record reps and label folks. When a new album dropped, Rene was always the guy pushing for that radio play. So, when I saw his name pop up, I figured it had something to do with music. But it wasn't about an album or mixtape this time.

50 was officially launching Sire Spirits, his luxury liquor brand. Branson Cognac and Le Chemin Du Roi Champagne were about to hit the Dallas market, and they were looking for DJ brand ambassadors—faces in the nightlife scene who could push the product authentically. Rene told me my name had come up.

What I didn't know at the time was how my name came up.

It was my guy Chris from Southside—he used to be 50's driver. He put the bug in people's ears. Told Lite, 50's barber, and some of the inner circle, "Yo, if y'all looking for somebody in Dallas, it's gotta be Kayotik. That's Reem. He from the neighborhood. He got the streets. He got the brand." They vouched for me when I didn't even know they were in the room.

That's divine favor right there. People speaking your name in rooms you're not in? That's God.

So, Rene gives me the rundown. They're bringing Sire Spirits to Dallas, doing an exclusive launch at The Statler Hotel. All the movers and shakers would be there—tastemakers, influencers, promoters, top-tier bartenders. Invite only. Rene said I'd be coming to "meet" 50 as part of the brand ambassador vetting process.

I laughed and told Rene: "Look, 50 ain't gonna know DJ Kayotik. But he gon' know Kareem Thomson."

Rene brushed it off like he's heard it all before. "Aight," he said, "we'll see."

That night, I pulled up to The Statler, suited up and sipping a Branson on the rocks. Worked the room a bit, then Rene gave me the look—it was time to go upstairs and meet 50.

I said it again on the way up: "He ain't gon' recognize the DJ name. Watch."

We walk in, Rene says, "50 Cent, meet DJ Kayotik."

50 looked at Rene. Then he looked at me.

"Nigga, that's Kareem Thomson—from my neighborhood!"

Rene lost it laughing. 50 dapped me up and said, "I remember when you told me in Chicago you was DJing. I see you really out here. They told me you was solid. Southside!"

Just like that, the deal was locked. I was officially one of the Sire Spirits DJ Brand Ambassadors.

I didn't need to prove nothing else. No resume. No pitch deck. No followers count. Real recognized real.

Being tapped as a brand ambassador for Sire Spirits was a blessing—but not everybody understood it.

As soon as I started posting on social media—thanking 50, talking about our childhood in Southside, posting behind-the-scenes flicks and brand content—folks started chirping. In the comments. In the DMs. Behind my back. "He don't really know 50 like that." "They just from the same hood." "Kayotik clout-chasin'." "He out here reaching."

Even some people I considered friends started questioning it. As if I needed to fabricate ties to another man to validate myself. I never needed 50 Cent to make me relevant—I was DJ Kayotik before the endorsement. But that didn't stop the rumors.

Surprisingly, one of the doubters was my own wife.

It wasn't malicious—Vanessa never hated or disrespected the connection. She just didn't think it was as deep as I said it was. She thought I was "playing it up" like everybody else online does for status.

That changed one weekend in Houston.

We were down there for a Sire Spirits activation at the Post Oak Hotel, working with their staff on new cocktails, training bartenders, and getting the brand in front of tastemakers. Vanessa came with me. That weekend included dinners with the team, DJ sets, and of course, 50. One night, we were sitting around a dinner table with Fif, his lawyer Steve, and a few others from the inner circle.

Steve looked over at me and asked, "You really grew up with Curtis?"

You know lawyers love to say the government name.

I replied, "Yeah. Me and Boo Boo go back. Southside Jamaica Queens. Like back-back. Boxing at the White House. Dirt mounds. Him betting on me while I hooped on the block."

I was sharing real stories—not industry tales, not fan fiction. These were childhood memories. And you could see it on 50's face—he remembered all of it.

Then Vanessa looked at him and asked, "You really know him, huh?"

50 laughed. "Yeah! That's my guy. We from the same neighborhood. We go way back."

She just stared at me.

When we got back to our room, I asked her, "So what made you ask him that?"

She said, "I ain't gonna lie… I knew you knew him… but I didn't think you really knew him like that."

We both laughed. I said, "You thought I was faking it too?"

She shook her head and smiled. "Not faking… just exaggerating."

And that's when it hit me: Even the people closest to you can't always see the full picture God's painting for your life—until they witness it for themselves.

It was all love. And from that moment on, Vanessa never questioned the bond again.

But our connection wasn't just personal. It was spiritual.

In 2008, my Moms was deep in the church, fully walking with God. She'd joined Holy Unity Christian Church in Jamaica, Queens. That's the same church 50's grandmother, Ms. Beulah Jackson—may she rest in peace—was a spiritual leader at. They became close friends.

When 50's grandparents renewed their vows at his massive estate—Mike Tyson's former mansion in Connecticut—my Moms was one of the church members invited. I later showed 50 a photo of him with my mother from that day. He remembered her instantly. "Yo, she talked to me for like ten minutes at the house," he said. And when I sent him a picture of his grandmother from that same day—a photo he had never seen before—he was visibly moved. Said it was like finding a lost memory.

You see, this wasn't just about me spinning records or pushing product. It wasn't just about childhood nostalgia or brand alignment. This was purpose. This was full-circle. This was God.

Being a brand ambassador for Sire Spirits didn't just look good on paper—it saved my life in real time.

Before the Branson and Le Chemin Du Roi deal, I was getting by—but barely. $52,000 a year as a morning show producer wasn't cutting it, especially not with a wife, two kids, and grown man responsibilities. The clubs weren't really moving like that anymore. Gigs were inconsistent. And as proud as I was to be on air, I wasn't proud of how light my checks felt after taxes.

So I humbled myself—again.

I started driving Uber.

Yep. DJ Kayotik, the voice on the radio, the guy on billboards and branded station trucks, was pulling up in a rental Hyundai to take you to work or brunch. I didn't care. I wasn't too good to hustle.

During the holidays, I knew my girls deserved a good Christmas. So I made it happen. I found out that Hertz had a program for Uber drivers—you rent the car, they deduct the cost from your earnings, and whatever's left is yours. I needed wheels, and they gave me a route.

And I'm not ashamed to admit it: I was grateful. Because I knew how it felt to have no car. To be homeless. To be down to your last dollar. So if I had to Uber by day and produce a morning show by early morning, so be it. I was a husband and a father first. DJ second.

At that time, Branson hadn't even hit full stride in the city yet. But once that Sire Spirits deal got finalized, everything shifted.

The money came in. The pressure eased up.

I didn't have to Uber anymore.

Not only was I making more in 6 months as a brand ambassador than I made all year at the station, but it gave me options. Options to choose which gigs to take. To spend more time with my family. To be present for the life I was building, instead of constantly hustling just to stay above water.

Vanessa noticed the difference. The girls noticed it. I had balance. I had time. I had some peace again.

Then, just as things started settling… the world shut down.

COVID hit in 2020, and the streets went silent.

The clubs were closed. Events were canceled. Outside was gone. Every brand ambassador, every DJ, every artist, bartender, promoter—we were all scrambling to figure out what came next.

And once again, 50 Cent came through.

Instead of letting the brand go cold or pausing the deal, 50 doubled down. He told us, "Keep working. Pivot to digital." He paid out the entire six-month contract—in full. And then extended it to a year.

While so many people were trying to keep their heads above water, I had the blessing of stability. I could provide. Keep food in the fridge. Keep the girls engaged. We didn't have to panic.

We got creative instead.

I set up a DJ booth in the house and turned our living room into a nightclub. We called it "Club Cabin Fever." I hung up the Branson and Le Chemin Du Roi banners in the background, dimmed the lights, fired up Instagram Live—and spun records while my daughters and Vanessa danced around the house like it was an actual club.

We laughed. We danced. We made memories.

I still remember Jayla requesting songs like she was in the middle of a real function. Jewel would bring snacks like it was bottle service. Vanessa turned into the party starter. And all while I was promoting the brand online and earning a full check from Sire Spirits.

At a time when most folks were spiraling, we were staying connected. Staying sane. Staying in motion.

That Thanksgiving, Vanessa came up with a wild idea—"Let's rent an RV and drive to the Grand Canyon."

At first, I was like, huh? An RV? Who do we think we are? But when she broke it down—no hotels, full kitchen on board, our own beds, safe travels—it made perfect sense.

So, we did it.

Fifteen hours on the road. Stopping at campgrounds. Cooking on a grill. Hugging our daughters under the Grand Canyon sunset. A kid from Southside Jamaica, Queens, spending Thanksgiving in an RV with his family at one of the wonders of the world. You can't make that up.

That trip changed me. It reminded me that God has always been in control—even when I felt like I was drowning. He gave me the tools, the favor, and the family to keep going.

By 2023, the world was back outside.

The pandemic was in the rearview. Clubs were packed again. Brands were back in motion. And my role as a DJ brand ambassador for Sire Spirits was rolling strong. I was getting booked more, taking better care of my body, and re-centering my focus on family first, business second.

But radio? That was another story.

The Veda Loca Morning Show was gone. Canceled in 2020. Veda and Jazzi Black were let go, and while Kruz shifted to mid-days, I was back in my old role—producing a syndicated morning show again. This time it was The Morning Hustle.

Same button pushing. Same four hours. Same routine. No growth.

I was stagnant.

I'd reached the ceiling. There was nothing else left for me to accomplish in radio unless it was leading my own local morning show—which wasn't happening. So I made myself a promise:

"By the time I turn 50, I'm leaving radio… unless God opens a new door."

I wasn't about to be one of those people clinging to something just because it was comfortable. I'd already been stripped of comfort plenty of times. I knew how to pivot. And now I had the faith to do it with boldness.

In the meantime, I poured myself into DJing and branding. I started securing new opportunities. I was selective, intentional. Still promoting Branson. Still repping Le Chemin Du Roi. Still working hard to build my foundation into something legacy-worthy.

And then came The Final Lap Tour.

When 50 announced he was hitting the road to celebrate the 20th anniversary of Get Rich or Die Tryin', I was genuinely happy for him. The fact that an album dropped two decades prior still had enough power to sell out arenas worldwide? That's legacy. And I knew it would be massive.

But I also knew I wasn't part of it.

I had DJ'd a few of his Texas shows here and there—San Antonio, Dallas, small spot dates when his DJ couldn't travel. But I wasn't in the official tour lineup. I wasn't his "tour DJ." I didn't expect to be. He'd had the same DJ for over ten years.

Still, something in me stirred. So I called Rene.

"If there's any opportunity for me to join the tour—even just to open a few dates—I'd love to be considered."

I said it humbly. Genuinely. And left it there.

But Vanessa? She wasn't leaving anything to chance. She hit her knees and went into full-on prayer mode.

"God, open the door. Let my husband be seen. Put his name in the right room."

She wasn't just praying for me to open. She was praying for me to be on the tour. Period.

I thought I was dreaming too big just asking to open a few sets. Vanessa believed I was thinking too small.

The tour kicked off July 21.

I didn't get a call.

But I was still following. Watching from a distance. Happy for my brother. Celebrating him. Not hating. Just waiting.

About a month later, Rene hit me up.

"50 wants you to come to the Atlanta show. Just watch."

That was all he said.

"Is everything cool?" I asked.

"Yea. Just watch the show."

So I booked a flight. Packed a bag. And told Vanessa, "He said to come watch."

"This is it," she said. "This is your moment. I feel it."

The show was at Cellairis Amphitheater in Atlanta, August 17.

I sat in the crowd and studied every move. I watched how the music hit. How 50 moved. Where the DJ dropped in, where he didn't. What songs worked. What didn't. I wasn't just watching—I was preparing.

After the show, I went backstage to dap 50 up.

"You saw the show?"

"Yea. Incredible. Proud of you."

"Good! Because if this DJ keeps f*ckin' up... I'm replacing him."

Then he turned and walked away.

His DJ was standing right behind me.

We locked eyes.

Awkward.

But in that moment, I knew something had just shifted.

I didn't say a word.

Not to the DJ, not to anyone.

But inside? I was on fire.

Fif had just told me, straight up, "You're next if this dude keeps slipping." And that meant one thing: I had to be ready. Not kinda ready. Locked in. Laser focused. Studied up. No excuses.

So I did what I always do when it's time to step up: I went to work.

I called my guy Krewsade, 50's videographer and someone I had built a real bond with. I told him, "I need the full show—every song, every transition, every cue."

He put me in touch with the team, and they delivered.

Every tour stop. Every set. Every camera angle. I watched like it was game film.

I broke it down song by song. Where the drops hit. Where 50 would walk across the stage. Where he wanted silence. Where he wanted the crowd hype. Where he needed space to breathe.

I knew the show inside and out before I ever touched a turntable.

I wasn't waiting on a shot—I was preparing for it.

Then came the Dallas show on August 25. Right in my city.

By then, I had heard whispers. That the DJ and 50 weren't clicking. The chemistry was off. Transitions were slipping. Cues were getting missed.

But when the Dallas show came? Everything looked like it had been patched up. 50 was on point. No public issues. The crowd was rocking.

Still, I didn't give up hope. I knew what I'd heard. And I knew God don't close doors without cracking windows.

Plus, Vanessa never stopped praying. She told me again before the show, "I still feel it. You're gonna be on this tour."

That night, I brought my daughters, Jewel and Jayla, to their first concert. They had never seen anything like it. And when I told them we were going backstage to meet "Uncle 50," their jaws hit the floor.

Jewel—who barely lets me hug her—got a kiss on the cheek from 50, and she didn't wipe it off for a week. We still laugh about that moment. It was like she met Michael Jackson.

"Daddy… that's really your friend?!"

It was one of the best nights of our lives. But I still wasn't on the tour.

Not yet.

Then came August 31st.

I was DJing in Dubai for Set Network's annual Labor Day events. Touring internationally, repping the brand, stacking opportunities. I was busy. Focused. Blessed.

That same night?

50 fired his DJ.

On stage.

Publicly.

It happened in Chula Vista, California—a suburb of San Diego. 50 was yelling for the DJ to drop a record… and nothing happened. Cue missed. Energy blown.

Finally, the DJ dropped the track.

But it was too late.

"STOP," Fif said. "I'm not f*ckin' with you. You getting outta here."

And just like that, the spot was open.

Next morning in Dubai—11am my time—I got a call.

Steve, 50's general counsel.

"We need you to come to Cali."

"When?"

"Yesterday."

I froze.

The door wasn't cracked anymore...

It was wide open.

When I hung up with Steve, I stood there for a second.

No music. No crowd noise. Just me, holding my phone, heart racing.

I got the call.

The call every DJ dreams of. The opportunity that could shift everything.

But there was a problem—I was in Dubai. And not just on vacation or chillin'. I was booked, DJing for an international event I had done three years straight. They took care of me, so I had to take care of them. It wasn't in me to just pack up and leave mid-gig.

So I did the only thing that made sense.

I called Vanessa.

It was 1AM in Dallas. She was knocked out. I whispered into the phone:

"Wake up, baby. I got the call."

She sat straight up.

"YOU GOT THE CALL?! I KNEW IT!! I told you! I told you this was it!"

We both sat in that moment—me in the Middle East, her in Texas—crying, praying, celebrating. Vanessa had been praying this into existence for months. She wanted it more than I did. She never wavered in her faith.

She jumped out of bed and got straight to work, pulling up flights, checking options.

But as much as I wanted to hop on the first plane back, I had to finish what I started in Dubai. I wasn't about to ghost a team that had invested in me. The same God who opened this door would also give me the grace to walk through it the right way.

So, we made the plan.

I'd honor the rest of my Dubai booking, then fly straight to Seattle, where 50 and the tour would be next.

The show was September 7, and I landed in Seattle on the 6th.

I stepped off that plane with no sleep, no heavy coat—just swim trunks, shorts, and Dubai heat still on my skin.

My first stop?

The mall.

I needed a tour-ready wardrobe. Remember: I'd gone from DJing in the desert to DJing a global stadium tour with one of the biggest artists on the planet.

God was funny like that.

Seattle was rainy and cool—typical Northwest vibes. I was exhausted but laser-focused. I had studied the show. I knew the cues. I knew where every drop should hit, every transition should glide. Still, nothing could prepare me for what that first night on stage would feel like.

I wasn't just DJing a club or opening for an artist.

I was about to control the sound for Curtis '50 Cent' Jackson, in front of a sold-out crowd, on a tour celebrating the 20th anniversary of one of the most iconic rap albums of all time. After speaking with 50, he suggested I watch a few more shows in person and prepare for my debut show on 9/11 in Edmonton, Canada. That advice gave me both relief and focus—it meant I had a little more time to study, to sharpen my timing, and to really understand the rhythm of the tour before stepping into that role myself.

That night, in Edmonton, I prayed hard.

Before soundcheck, I walked backstage, found a quiet corner, and gave it to God:

"Lord, if this is where I'm supposed to be, give me peace. Guide my hands. Steady my nerves. Let me serve my purpose on this stage tonight."

Then it was go-time.

50 walked in, looked at me, and said simply:

"Let's do this."

No speech. No prep talk. Just trust. He had seen the work, and he knew I was ready.

When the lights dimmed and that beat for "What Up Gangsta" dropped, I was the one behind the boards. The energy exploded. It wasn't just sound—it was electricity. Every transition hit. Every drop landed. Every cue was sharp. Fif turned around a couple times and gave me the nod. That was all I needed.

By the time we hit "Many Men," the crowd was singing so loud I couldn't hear myself in the headphones. And I didn't need to. I was locked in. Tunnel vision. Pure motion.

After the show, 50 pulled me aside.

"That's how it's supposed to feel."

I smiled. Not too wide. Just enough. Because this wasn't luck. This was divine alignment. This was legacy meeting preparation. I wasn't just 50's new DJ.

I was home.

Tour life hit different when it's for something this big. Every city, every night, we lit the stage on fire. From Seattle to Sacramento, LA to London. We touched countries I never imagined I'd see—Germany, Amsterdam, Australia, and more. And in every venue, every stadium, every arena… I showed up not just as DJ Kayotik, but as the man who survived.

I survived heartbreak.

I survived hunger.

I survived betrayal.

I survived the death of my son.

And now? I was thriving in front of thousands. With my brother from Southside Jamaica Queens. 50 Cent didn't just save my life—he gave me a second one.

What made it even more powerful is that I didn't have to fake anything. I didn't have to chase clout or pretend to be someone I wasn't. I got this opportunity by being me. The same Kareem from Rochdale who had the courage to show up in every room God called him to.

Each night on tour was a redemption story. My sets weren't just beats and transitions. They were therapy. They were my grief. My healing. My hustle. My joy. They were me talking to Dante, letting him know:

"You didn't leave this Earth in vain. Everything you dreamed of—DJing big stages, touring, making a name—I'm doing it for us now."

There were moments I'd step away after a set, headphones still hanging around my neck, and cry. Not out of sadness—but out of awe. Because God really did it. He took my lowest point—burying my son—and used it to elevate my purpose.

I felt Dante's presence with me on every flight. In every prayer circle. During every soundcheck. Before every set. I could feel him on stage beside me, vibing out. Smiling. Rocking with the crowd. The Final Lap Tour wasn't just 50 Cent's celebration.

It was my resurrection.

When I returned home in between tour legs, my daughters looked at me differently. Not because I was DJing for a global superstar—but because I was present. Focused. Healed enough to give them the version of me they deserved.

And Vanessa? She was proud. But more than that—she was relieved. Because she saw the man she loved come back to life. She saw the husband she believed in—finally walk in his full power.

They say tour ends when the stage lights fade, the merch is packed, and the buses go dark. But for me, the real tour was just beginning. Every city we hit, every soul I touched with music, was proof that **your pain doesn't disqualify you—**it prepares you.

And so now, when people ask what chapter this is in my life?

I tell them:

"It's the legacy tour. For Dante. For me. For every broken soul that refused to stay broken."

Because the music never stops.

And neither will I.

CHAPTER 15
"THE FINAL LAP"

My first day on tour felt like the first day of boot camp.

Only this time, instead of having my brother Bunkin with me, I had Tony Yayo and Uncle Murda. Yayo, being from Southside too, welcomed me with open arms. Murda was happy I was there—he was honestly just tired of the other DJ messing up.

The A Party—Fif, Yayo, Murda, Fif's barber Lite, and the tour manager—was glad to see me. But the B Party made me feel like I was back on my ship in the Navy, being sized up like an outsider. And just like the first day on that ship, wasn't nobody scaring me. And I damn sure wasn't about to get stuffed into a dryer.

To be fair, I understood the energy. The B Party—the band and dancers—were tight-knit. They'd been with Fif for over a decade and were used to how things had always been. I was the new guy, and worse, I was about to replace someone from their inner circle. So of course they were looking at me sideways.

I heard the whispers: "That's the DJ replacing our guy... only because he's from Southside."

"That's 50's boy. They go way back."

There was no mention of the mistakes the previous DJ had been making. No acknowledgment of my skill set. Just the assumption that I was there because 50 Cent was doing his homeboy a favor.

But anyone who really knew Fif should've known better. He don't hand out favors. And what other people thought? That wasn't my concern.

I had been counted out before. White Gary, the assistant program director at K104, didn't think I'd ever be good enough to be a full-time jock. So I quit. And became a member of a morning show at 97.9 The Beat.

They didn't have to believe in me.

I believed in God.

I believed in myself.

And I believed in Fif.

I was there to do a job.

That first day, I focused on getting acclimated. Got my Final Lap Tour badge so I could move freely backstage. Met the security team, production crew, and tour manager—just soaking in the lay of the land and learning how all the moving parts worked. Instead of studying videos Krewsade helped me collect, I was now watching it all in real-time.

I was excited. I was focused. And I stayed guarded. I didn't know yet who would rock with me and who wouldn't.

To be honest, I don't think the previous DJ believed he was really getting let go. DJ Whoo Kid, Fif's first DJ, had been fired and brought back multiple times. So maybe he figured he'd be back soon, too. But that kind of comfort is what caused him to lose the spot in the first place.

Me? I could never get comfortable. Not after everything I'd been through.

I still remember hustling outside of Key Foods, hoping to make ten bucks after twelve hours. Splitting twenty "murder burgers" with Randy and Bunkin because it was all we could afford. Losing my house. Sleeping in my truck. Sleeping on floors where I wasn't always welcome. You think I was gonna take this opportunity for granted?

Never.

I didn't even have a passport until I got married. And now? That passport was about to get more stamps than the Post Office.

The previous DJ was cool, though. I've got no ill will toward him. We said what's up. It was cordial. Brief. No drama. But while he may not have known what was coming, I did.

So I stayed ready.

We left Seattle and headed to Canada—first Vancouver, then Calgary.

My debut show?

September 11, 2023. Edmonton, Alberta, Canada.

I was up early that morning. First thing I did, like I do every morning, was pray.

Then I hit the gym for a couple hours, followed by an hour in the sauna. After breakfast at the hotel, I checked in with my mother and Vanessa. I was excited. Nervous. Focused. Ready.

I even posted on social media that this was my debut show. It felt surreal.

September 11.

On that date in 2001, New York City was under attack. That day, I rushed to get my son from daycare, just twenty minutes from where the third plane hit the Pentagon. I was frantically waiting for my mom to call and let me know she was okay. Watching chaos unfold on the news. Praying for every family whose lives were changed forever.

On April 4, 2015, I lost my son. And with him, I lost myself.

But now, on September 11, 2023, something came full circle. After everything—leaving a six-figure salary to chase purpose, stepping away from radio, trusting God when it made no sense—I was about to hit one of the biggest stages in the world with one of the biggest hip-hop artists of all time.

It was showtime.

Sound check wasn't until 4:00 p.m., so we met in the lobby around 3:30. With shows like this, we always had to arrive hours early to test everything—the mics, the audio, the lighting, even the "magic box" Fif popped out of at the top of the show. That thing had to work flawlessly.

Venues typically had built-in catering, so meals were covered. The show itself didn't start until 9:00 p.m. After sound check, we had downtime to chill, regroup, and lock in.

Everyone had their own green room. Fif had his. Yayo and Murda had theirs. The band had theirs. The previous DJ used to hang with the band, so that was their guy. But me? I came in with a different energy. I saw myself as an artist now. I spent most of my time in the room with Yayo, Murda—or Fif himself.

Yayo and Murda? They smoked all day. That weed smoke? Thick. I didn't know yet how that would affect me, but I'd learn soon enough.

This sound check was different. Before, I had been shadowing. Watching. Learning. But now? I was behind the wheel. I was driving the car.

And even with the pressure, I didn't feel overwhelmed.

I had prepared in prayer.

Vanessa had prayed over me.

My mom had covered me.

I was surrounded by divine protection.

Yayo pulled me to the side and kept it 100 with me:

"Don't fuck up. We know 50 brought you here for a reason. You his man. But don't fuck up."

That's facts. And I wasn't worried. I knew exactly what I came to do.

The only ones still skeptical were the band members. And I understood why—they were loyal to their guy. But I also knew something they didn't: when God places you in a room, no one else's opinion matters.

Yayo always said, "Kayotik is a praying man."

And he was right.

I wasn't walking in confident.

I was walking in GODfident.

This moment wasn't even about me.

I never saw myself touring the world as a stadium DJ. But you know who did?

Dante.

DJ Kidd.

He used to tell me he wanted to be a big-time DJ one day. He had big dreams. Now I was living them. Every night, when I hit that stage, it wasn't just Kayotik out there. It was us. My son, my motivator, my angel. Dante was taking the stage through me.

This was his tour.

So, I showed up. And I showed out.

The arena was sold out—20,000 people strong. The lights were low. The energy was electric. The countdown began.

I was nervous. No lie. I had seen this same venue empty just hours before. Now it was packed wall to wall. All eyes were about to be on me and Fif. But once the music dropped, something clicked. That switch flipped.

We were in the zone.

For the first hour of the show, I knew the exact order of the songs—tracks 1 through 19. Then came the encore, and that was my moment.

See, that's when Fif would leave the stage. The lights would go dim. The crowd would go wild. And it was my job to control the energy, bring the people higher, and signal that we weren't done yet.

"Y'all want some more 50 Cent?! Nah—I said, make some motherfucking noise!"

Then I'd lead the crowd in chanting:

"50 Cent… 50 Cent… 50 Cent…"

And right at the peak, I'd drop the beat—and Fif would re-emerge. The arena would erupt. That's how we did it. Night after night.

I wish I could tell you I soaked it all in that first show… but truthfully, I was laser-focused. Locked in. I had something to prove—to the team, to Fif, and to myself.

I give myself a B+ on that debut. The crowd rocked with me. There were no complaints. But I'm my own worst critic. My scratches could've been cleaner. My ad-libs could've had more fire. My hands were sweaty. I was nervous. But I got through it.

And then—I lost my voice.

Yeah. Completely gone.

I hadn't been doing clubs regularly in the same way I used to. I'd been on radio, talking in short bursts—30 to 60 seconds at a time. Not screaming for 90 straight minutes in front of a packed arena. I wasn't using my diaphragm like I should've been. I was yelling from the throat. And it caught up to me.

Tea wasn't helping. Rest wasn't doing enough.

After just one night of proving myself, I felt like the rug was getting pulled from under me. The enemy was attacking.

I'd just had my breakthrough… now my voice—my tool—was under assault.

The next couple of shows were rough. I struggled through them. Yayo and Murda noticed and started coaching me:

"Save your voice for the encore."

"Skip the ad-libs."

"We need you to be good when it counts."

Even when I tried to hype the crowd, Yayo would shoot me a look like, "Cut it out." He was looking out for me.

But Winnipeg was the worst.

I hit the stage and tried to project—but nothing came out. I was squeaky, strained, nearly mute. And I'll never forget it: the band was laughing. Laughing. At me. Right there on stage.

I was livid. Embarrassed. Hurt.

Here I was… this close to fulfilling my life's purpose, and I'm out there croaking like a frog. I was ready to fight everyone backstage. Every emotion hit me at once—anger, shame, fear, disappointment. But I held it together.

Because Vanessa was praying.

Because my Moms was praying.

Because I had already come too far.

I asked God to protect me. Heal me. Strengthen me. I knew I was under attack. But I also knew: I was supposed to be here.

A week or so later, Fif pulled me aside at the gym. He was in the sauna and called me in.

"Yo, what the fuck is up with your voice?"

It was raspy as hell, but I answered, "I don't know, bro. I'm working on it. Drinking tea, staying hydrated. I'ma get it together."

And then he gave it to me straight:

"Kareem, I need you to get your voice together. This ain't like when we was growing up in Southside. This ain't a hard job. You're not doing construction. You're not breaking your back. I need you to give me 90 flawless minutes. That's it. Just an hour and a half of work. I took a chance on you, because I believe in you. Don't make me regret it."

That conversation hit me deep. I respected it. No sugarcoating, no ego. Just accountability and opportunity.

And that's what real brothers do.

I told him, "I got you. I won't let you down."

He even offered to bring in a doctor to give me a B-12 shot. I was open to anything. The doctor also let me know that all that second-hand smoke from Yayo and Murda wasn't helping my vocal cords either. Go figure.

Through that moment, I felt covered. I felt supported. And gradually—my voice started to return.

The biggest challenge on tour wasn't my voice—it was being away from my family.

Thanksgiving 2023? I wasn't sitting at a dinner table with Vanessa and the girls, passing plates and laughing over memories. I was in Zallaq, Bahrain, standing behind the turntables, asking the crowd if they wanted more 50 Cent.

That was the part of this dream that no one prepares you for.

Yes, the travel was incredible. Yes, the crowds were wild. Yes, I was living out my and my son's shared dream. But that didn't take away the ache of missing cheer games, school plays, nightly prayers, or morning hugs. My foundation—Vanessa, Jewel, and Jayla—is what keeps me grounded. And without them, it didn't matter how many private jets I flew on or how many five-star hotels I stayed in.

Ten or fifteen years ago, I couldn't have said that.

Back then, my foundation was ambition. Survival. Proving I wasn't my father. Getting to the bag. Now? Now I saw life differently. It's God. Then family. Then the rest. That order keeps everything in alignment.

When the schools reopened after COVID, I started a new tradition. No matter where I was—on tour, at home, or overseas—I'd pray with my girls every weekday morning. I'd pray over Vanessa. I'd speak protection and love over them. I'd say:

"Jewel and Jayla, you are my beautiful Black princesses."

"Vanessa, you are my beautiful Black queen."

And they'd smile. Even on the road, I made sure they felt me close. Because I know what absence feels like. I lived it growing up. I vowed my children would never have to wonder if their daddy was proud of them, or if he was present.

This tour wasn't about me anymore.

The selfish hunger for spotlight had been replaced by gratitude and purpose. I wasn't chasing fame—I was honoring legacy.

Of course, there were some incredible perks to being on tour with an A-list artist.

Let's start with the travel. For the European leg, we had a beautiful charter bus. When we traveled to Saudi Arabia and a few other international spots, we flew commercial. But most of the time?

Private jets.

Yeah, PJs. Just like the song.

The kid who used to stand outside Key Foods hustling for car fare... was now stepping on private jets, laptop open, flying city to city, country to country with 50 Cent. There were maybe 10–12 of us on board. Fif, Yayo, Uncle Murda, me, security, Krewsade, his assistants, and the tour manager. No pretzels. No half cup of ginger ale. You want tea with honey? You got it. Champagne? Right there. Caesar salad? Say less.

I didn't take a second of it for granted.

I'll be honest—every city, I wanted to snap a photo on that jet. But I didn't want to look like a tourist. So every now and then I'd tap Krewsade or Jeremy and have them get a flick. Just enough for the memories.

That's the thing about being the new guy on tour—you're the only one who hasn't lived this life yet. But I embraced it fully.

I had my laptop open on every flight, ready to go over the show with Fif or the team. The DJ before me wasn't doing that. He was exhausted, apparently. But how could I ever be tired when I prayed to be here? When I had begged God for this assignment?

We stayed in five-star hotels. The Ritz-Carlton. The Versace Hotel in Paris. I'm talking suites with views that made you tear up. This wasn't a vacation—it was a victory lap.

We'd have lunch at the venues, catered. Then after the show, they'd bring in whatever we wanted—Popeyes, Pappadeaux, you name it. You just had to pay your own room service tab. Because if you didn't? And the tour manager had to tell 50 you didn't square up?

Not a good look.

But I wasn't there to act brand new. I was there to honor God, honor Fif, and honor my son.

Before every show, I'd find a quiet space and pray for at least five to ten minutes. The stage managers got used to it. They knew if Kayotik hadn't taken the stage yet, it was because he was praying.

I'd pray over my daughters. Over Vanessa. Over Dante.

"God, thank you for this gift. For this calling. For this moment. Use me. Let me honor my son. Let me live this dream loud. And let me return it all back to you."

There were so many unforgettable moments on tour, but December 14 into December 15, 2023, in Auckland, New Zealand, will forever be etched in my soul.

That night, we were performing at Spark Arena, New Zealand's largest indoor arena. That same stage has seen legends—Beyoncé, Taylor Swift, Red Hot Chili Peppers. Now, it was our turn. 50 Cent. DJ Kayotik.

But for me, it was more than a big stage. It was deeply personal.

On December 14, 2014, my son Dante had posted an image to Instagram of a DJ standing on his turntables in front of a massive, sold-out crowd. The caption read:

"Real life goals. Give me another year."

He was dreaming out loud. And even though he wasn't physically here, I was determined to bring that dream to life. For him. Through me.

So I did.

That night, as "Many Men" prepared to drop, I cued the crowd.

"New Zealand! Get them cell phones out right now! From the front to the back, light this bitch up! Light it up! More lights, more lights!"

And they lit it up.

Every single hand was in the air. Lights everywhere. Phones waving, a sea of stars in the dark.

And I stood on the turntables.

I had on my custom LLTK chain—"Long Live The Kidd." I panned from the crowd to myself and let the moment breathe. Then dropped the track.

It was a full-circle moment. Dante's post… and me living it.

I put the video next to his Instagram picture and posted it. Vanessa got goosebumps. So did Nikita. Everyone who saw it did.

It was identical.

That wasn't just a moment for me. That was a spiritual release. A declaration. A tribute. A victory.

"Dante, we did it."

"I hope I'm making you proud, son."

"Your dreams didn't die. They're alive through me."

The Final Lap Tour would go on to make history.

We performed in front of capacity crowds of up to 100,000 people. It became only the third rap tour in history to gross over $100 million. A global success.

Kids from Southside Jamaica, Queens were now recognized across Europe, Asia, Australia, and beyond. There were countries where people didn't even speak English—but they knew 50 Cent songs. They knew DJ Kayotik.

In one city, fans were waiting by the PJ terminal. I don't know how they found us. But somebody had dug up an old photo of me and asked for an autograph. My first.

Yayo and the guys laughed, clowning me: "Ohhh shit, this nigga signing autographs now??"

But 50? He just smiled.

That moment was as proud for him as it was for me.

By the end of the tour, my relationship with 50 was stronger than ever—both personally and professionally. There was trust. Chemistry. Mutual respect. We'd moved from "here's your set list" to me texting him the full rundown before each show:

"Here's tonight's list—let me know if you want any changes."

Most of the time? No changes.

If I'm on FaceTime with Vanessa or the girls, Fif jumps in and says what's up. My daughters still call him Uncle 50. That's my boss. But that's my brother, too.

When the Final Lap Tour ended, I didn't know what was next. But I trusted God.

The last official show was December 21, 2023, in Abu Dhabi. I flew home just in time for Christmas, and we booked a family cruise to bring in the new year. We docked in Miami on New Year's Eve, and that night?

I DJ'd 50 Cent's show.

Tour or no tour—I was still his DJ. That's when I took "tour DJ" out of my bio. I was no longer filling in. This wasn't a one-time thing. This was the next chapter.

This was my calling.

December 15, 2024 became even more significant.

Exactly one year to the day of that show in New Zealand, I received an honorary doctorate from Leaders Esteem Christian Bible University. The same date. A divine alignment I couldn't have orchestrated if I tried.

The process? Someone nominates you, and then the school does their due diligence. My nomination came from Dr. K.C. Fox. Crazy part? I knew her back when there was no "Dr." in front of her name. She was the producer for the TV segment of the Veda Loca Morning Show, and I was the radio producer sending her clips to review. She's watched my journey from the radio booth… to the world stage.

Leaders Esteem is an accredited Christian university based out of Houston. Rickey Smiley—the same man whose show I used to push buttons for—is also an alumnus. The same man who hugged me when I broke down in the studio after Dante's death.

This recognition meant everything. You do all this work… endure all this pain… and hope somebody sees it. To be honored for that work? It was one of the proudest moments of my life.

And the only graduation my Moms had ever seen me at was high school.

So, I flew her and my stepdad out for this one.

She got to see me go from Kareem Thomson to Dr. Kareem "DJ Kayotik" Thomson.

Do I feel worthy of it? Honestly—no. There's so much more to do. But it put a battery in my back to go even harder. Because God ain't done with me yet.

This book was part of that purpose. A divine assignment. And now that it's complete, I feel like I'm just getting started.

2024 was all business.

I transitioned from DJ Kayotik the sole proprietor… to DJ Kayotik, LLC.

The Kayotik Foundation, founded in 2011, is now an official 501(c)(3) nonprofit. I've been laying the foundation—literally and spiritually—brick by brick. Everything I've been through was preparing me to build this house. Not just the metaphorical one… the actual one, too.

Vanessa and I bought several acres of land by the same lake where Dante passed. I didn't know how close it was to the exact location where they found him. But God did. In 2025, I plan to start building a legacy home in my son's honor.

After the Final Lap Tour, we purchased property in Shreveport, Louisiana—home of the second-largest Black-owned TV and film production studio in the country. Owned by Curtis "50 Cent" Jackson. I told Fif about the investment, and he checked it out and said, "It's a good buy."

That conversation actually led him to buy all the land he now owns in Shreveport. I believed in him and in his vision—and like he always says:

"If you bet on me, it's a sure win."

Just Google "Humor & Harmony Weekend Shreveport." That's only the beginning of what he's building there.

To close out the year?

We brought Vegas to life.

December 27–31 and January 3–4, 2025, we had a Vegas residency at Planet Hollywood Resort and Casino.

I've DJ'd in Vegas before. At Drai's After Hours. For Jardin, the dispensary I'm a brand ambassador for. I even did a show with Cardi B. But this? This was the biggest stage I'd ever touched in that city.

The same kid who turned down a fight at Madison Square Garden because I didn't feel ready…

…was now rocking stadiums around the globe with 50 Cent.

That's God.

This may be the last chapter of this book. But my story? Far from over.

My son once posted a DJ pic with the caption:

"Real life goals. Give me another year."

And while his DJ name didn't have an acronym—just DJ Kidd for Dante—I've come to realize what it truly stands for now:

DJ KIDD = Kayotik Is Dante's Dream.

And I'm living that dream out loud—on every stage, with every beat, and every breath I take... until I see my son again.

Long Live The Kidd.

ABOUT THE AUTHOR

Dr. Kareem "DJ Kayotik" Thomson is a powerhouse in music, entertainment, and culture. With more than two decades of experience behind the turntables, he is renowned for his electrifying presence, unmatched mixing skills, and a deep connection to the culture he represents.

As the official celebrity DJ for hip-hop legend 50 Cent, Kayotik has performed across more than 30 countries, captivating audiences of all sizes with his high-energy sets that blend hip-hop, R&B, and Top 40 hits. His journey—from the streets of Jamaica, Queens, to international stages—is a testament to his relentless work ethic and unwavering commitment to excellence.

Now based in Dallas, Texas, DJ Kayotik is more than just a performer—he's a visionary leader and community advocate. He is the founder of the Kayotik Foundation, a nonprofit organization focused on empowering underserved communities through music education, mentorship, and social outreach. In 2024, his impact was nationally recognized with an Honorary Doctorate of Philosophy in Humanitarianism and the Presidential Lifetime Achievement Award from President Joe Biden.

His influence also spans the airwaves, where he has served as a respected voice in radio—introducing emerging talent, breaking records, and remaining a trusted source for what's next in music and culture.

Whether rocking sold-out arenas, mentoring the next generation, or leading community initiatives, Dr. Kayotik brings passion, integrity, and purpose to everything he does. A dynamic storyteller and speaker, his voice—shaped by adversity, faith, and resilience—continues to inspire others to overcome life's trials and build a legacy that matters.

www.ingramcontent.com/pod-product-compliance
Lightning Source LLC
Chambersburg PA
CBHW071238130626
46556CB00003B/1072